# *Follow!*

## Making Disciples Jesus' Way

**Trinity Lutheran Church**

# Contents

# Introduction

## Remembering the Main Thing

What is the purpose of the Christian life? What is our driving mission? If you were to ask Jesus, I think he would probably answer using the following words:

*"All authority in heaven and on earth has been given to me. Therefore go and make disciples of all nations, baptizing them in the name of the Father and of the Son and of the Holy Spirit, and teaching them to obey everything I have commanded you. And surely I am with you always, to the very end of the age."*

~Matthew 28:18–20 (NIV)

That's it.

The one thing that Jesus wants us to do, over and above everything else, is make disciples. Should everything else fall by the wayside, this one thing was to be the non-negotiable, all-encompassing drive of the church. It was his final instruction to his disciples and it remains his instruction to us as well. We are to be disciples who make disciples.

But what does that mean?

1

# Defining "Discipleship"

In the New Testament, the Greek word for "disciple" is *mathetes* (μαθητής). This word literally means "student" or "learner." In the ancient world disciples would follow a rabbi or religious leader, and the goal of discipleship was to become like the one you followed.

So disciples would not only study what their rabbi taught, but also how he lived, how he interacted with others, what he prioritized, and how he made decisions. In fact, they would study him so closely they would even take note of and try to mimic how he dressed, walked, slept, and ate. One ancient rabbinic blessing went something like this: "May you be covered in the dust of your rabbi." The idea was that you would follow your rabbi so closely that you would literally be covered in the dust that he kicked up as he walked.

So what does it mean to be a disciple of Jesus? Quite simply, a disciple of Jesus is someone who is a "life-long learner of Jesus."[1] He or she is a person who increasingly looks, lives, and loves more like Jesus. And like Jesus, he or she is also willing to help *others* grow as disciples.

The reason we do this is because it is what Jesus has called us to do. Nothing more. Nothing less.

---

# The Focus of This Study

And that brings us to the focus of this study. Over these six sessions you are going to have a chance to look specifically at how Jesus made disciples, in order that you might grow in your own walk with him, but also so that you can help others do the same.

Here is an outline of where we are going and what you can expect:

### Session 1: Unity in Diversity

We often forget how different the 12 disciples were. They came from different backgrounds politically and socioeconomically. Too

---

[1] See Mike Breen, *Building a Discipling Culture,* chapter 3.

often we as Christians are only willing to disciple those who are like us. In this session we will look at what it means to be a community that disciples everyone and draws us into relationships with people who are very different from us.

## Session 2: Speaking the Truth in Love

We cannot grow if we do not have someone willing to speak truth into our lives. And we cannot hear that truth unless it is spoken in love. This session will focus on truth, love, and accountability, and the important role that they play in the journey of a disciple.

## Session 3: Test Your Faith

Discipleship involves being tested and examining our faith to see where we are weak and how we can grow. This session will introduce you to a tool to guide you in taking your next steps as a follower of Jesus.

## Session 4: Try and Discuss

Discipleship involves trying what we have been taught, and then debriefing with the person who is discipling us. This basic model of "apprenticeship" was repeated again and again by Jesus with his disciples, and is meant to serve as a model for us in our own discipleship.

## Session 5: Witness—Sharing Our Faith

A key skill and job for every follower of Jesus is the ability to share our faith. We need to be able to tell others about the hope that we have in Christ Jesus. In this session, we will talk about a few simple ways to begin sharing your faith with those whom Jesus has placed in your life.

## Session 6: Share Your Life

Discipleship can only happen in an environment of love. Jesus commanded the disciples to love one another. For us to be a part of the family of God, and to disciple one another, we need to open up our lives, overcome fear, and share our lives with others. This session will address the importance of relationships and transparency in the process of discipleship.

In addition to your group time, you will have a chance to reflect on these subjects throughout your week through daily devotional time, reflecting on and putting into practice the lessons that you learned during your study.

## Our Approach

We are going to be using a method of Scripture study based on the *Biblical Equipping Model.*[2] This approach allows you to study any text of Scripture and apply it to your daily life. It encourages both group discussion (together) and personal application (apart).

The **Together** portion is what you will do when you are going through the study with your small group. The **Apart** portion will structure your daily time in God's Word and provide you with some guidance for how to continue living out the lessons you learned during your group study time.

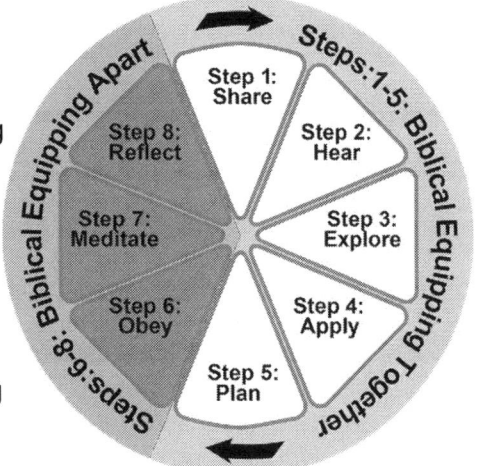

### TOGETHER

**Share:** Talk with your group about how God's Word has affected your life since your last group meeting.

**Hear:** Begin your study of the text with a moment of silence to open your heart to God's Word. Then listen together as the passage is read.

**Explore:** Study the passage as a group to learn what the passage meant to those who wrote and originally heard it.

---

2 Based on *Biblical Equipping: God's Word in Your World* by David A. Paap (Stephen Ministries, 1996).

**Apply:** Reflect on the passage and connect it to your own life. The goal of the application time is to ask: "What is God saying and what am I going to do in response?"

**Plan:** Conclude by making a conscious plan to apply the Word to your daily life over the course of the next week.

### APART

**Obey:** Respond to God's Word by living according to what you heard and learned during your group time.

**Meditate:** Set aside time to daily meditate on God's Word. Use a portion of the text that you studied during your group session and ponder it in your heart. What is God continuing to say to you through His Word?

**Reflect:** Think about how God is working in your life and how you are doing at living daily according to God's Word. Decide what experiences you wish to share with others at your next group meeting.

The goal of all our studies is not simply gaining head knowledge, but to apply God's truth to our lives. That is why this model has such a heavy emphasis on both study *and* application.

Our desire is that God's Word would truly shape your life and help you grow in the same values and behaviors as Jesus.

## Values & Behaviors

And speaking of values, let's talk a little bit about what those values are. Values are things that we care so much about that we do something with them. Values are always meant to shape behaviors.

We believe that there are really seven values that characterize what it means to be a disciple of Jesus. You might even say that these are "Jesus behaviors" that help us look, live, and love more like Him. Those values are...

### Worship

We live lives of worship and gratitude to God, both privately and in fellowship with other believers: This is why we worship weekly with the church, whenever possible. But we also cultivate daily time in prayer and the study of God's Word through personal devotions.

### Connect

You can't grow spiritually unless you are connected relation-ally. That is why we make being part of a small group such a high priority. A healthy small group is one that studies God's Word, is coached in and connected to the church's mission, and meets regularly (at least every other week).

### Serve

We seek to know our gifts and use them for the sake of helping others. We do this by serving both within our church community as well as out in the broader community where God has placed us.

### Generosity

Because God has been so generous with us, we joyfully give a tithe or beyond a tithe. Tithing means giving 10% off the top. But being generous is about more than a minimum percentage. It means we are also open to being generous wherever God gives us an oppor-tunity to do so.

### Leading

We are willing to be led and to use our gifts to lead others. Every-one needs the support, encouragement, and accountability that comes from being led by someone else. But it also means that we are called to lead for the sake of serving and mentoring others.

**Sharing**

We intentionally cultivate and have relationships with at least two people who are far from God. We all have people in our lives who don't yet follow Jesus. Committing to sharing means that we are actively praying for them, inviting them to church, and having regular spiritual conversations with them.

**Accountability**

We are willing to be held accountable for our own growth and leadership by others within the church family. Accountability means that we are willing to follow through on our commitments and receive the support and encouragement from others to do so. It means being transparent with those in our small group communities and our leadership teams about what is going on in our lives and where we could use encouragement and support.

As you work through these studies together, we want to encourage you to always evaluate your next steps in light of these values. How does the passage you are studying highlight one or more of these values? Which of the values is a next step you need to work on with God's help?

Our hope is that as you leave out these values and put into practice these "Jesus behaviors" you will grow as a disciple who makes disciples.

# Starting Your Journey

One final word before you dive into this study guide. Remember how the Great Commission ends. Jesus concludes his charge to the disciples with these words:

> *And surely I am with you always,*
> *to the very end of the age."*
>
> ~Matthew 28: 20 (NIV)

Your journey as a disciple is not one that you make alone. It is made in the company of fellow disciples, who are there to encourage, support, and equip you as you follow Christ. But it is also made in the company of Jesus, the one who promises to go with you always, even to the very end of the age.

So as you begin this journey, know that you aren't alone. Jesus is walking with you every step of the way to provide you with the hope and the power to follow him wherever he leads.

May God bless you as you embark on this study with your group.

# Unity in Diversity

*"We have a powerful myth in our culture,*
*the myth of the self-made man or woman.*
*But let's be honest. There's no such thing.*
*Success requires help—and usually lots of it."*
~Michael Hyatt

---

## Introduction

Welcome to your first study as a group! Over the next several weeks we are going to be talking about the importance of discipleship and learning what it means to look, live, and love more like Jesus.

But this is not a journey that we embark on alone. We need to be together in community. Why? Because that's the way God designed it. In fact, Solomon wrote the following about the importance of community.

*"Two are better than one, because they have a good*
*reward for their labor. If either of them falls down,*
*one can help the other up. But pity anyone who*
*falls and has no one to help them up...Though one*
*may be overpowered, two can defend themselves.*
*A cord of three strands is not easily broken."*
~Ecclesiastes 4:9–12

And this is where your group comes in. Over the next several weeks you will have a chance to get to know one another better, encourage each other in your respective walks with Jesus, and grow in your understanding of what it means to be His disciples.

But doing life together is not always easy. It will involve honest conversations, vulnerability, a readiness to listen, and perhaps even a bit of conflict. But that's okay. That is also how God designed it. Which is why this first study is going to focus on the theme of diversity and what it really means to live life together in community.

## Share

Usually in the *Share* portion of your study you will share how you have been growing as a disciple of Jesus since your last meeting. This will include reflecting on whatever application point you made last time as a response to what God was teaching you.

However, given that this is your first meeting, take some time to share the following with one another:

- How did you get connected to this group?
- Why did you decide to join?
- What do you hope to get out of your time together as a group?

Once you've had a chance to share, take a moment to pray for your time together, both now and over the course of the next several weeks.

## Hear

During the *Hear* portion of your group time, you want to take just a moment to quiet your hearts and just listen to the Word of God as it is read.

So, take a few seconds to just sit and be silent.

Then, have one person read *Mark 3:13–19.*

After the text has been read, just take another moment of silence and then play the *Session 1: Unity in Diversity* video.

Jesus was calling his disciples to both a _____ and

a _____.

Discipleship is as much about _____ Jesus as it is

about _____ Jesus.

You can't grow _____ unless you are connected

_____.

Jesus' disciples were diverse _____ and

_____.

Jesus knew that diversity was a _____ not a

_____.

Jesus knew that diversity was required for the sake of the

_____.

Jesus knew that diversity would be a clear marker of _____

_____.

## Explore

In the *Explore* section we are going to take a closer look at Mark
3:13–19 to discover what it means to those who wrote and originally
heard it.

1. Take a moment to consider again the diversity among Jesus' early disciples. One was a Zealot, another a tax collector. Some were wealthy while others were poor day laborers. Some lived their whole lives in Galilee while others may have come to Judea from places as far away as Syria.[3] What surprises you about this group of people that Jesus selects?

2. Imagine that you are one of the disciples being called. What would surprise you about your fellow disciples?

3. In the video, Pastor Nick noted that this is a group of men from different socioeconomic and political backgrounds. What possible challenges do you think they would have faced in terms of working together as a team? What barriers might have frustrated their attempts to form a cohesive community? What might they have learned, both about Jesus and about one another, as a result of their time "on the road" together?

4. How might their diversity, as a small group community, have actually been a strength in terms of achieving their mission?

## Apply

In the *Apply* section we are going to get a bit more personal as we consider the implications that this text has for our own lives.

---

[3] To learn more about these twelve men, their diversity and their eventual impact, see *Appendix 3: The Twelve Disciples.*

5. One of the things that Jesus highlights, from the very outset of his ministry, is that his community of disciples is *designed for diversity.* It is to be a place where people who wouldn't naturally hang out together become not only friends but family. What do you find appealing about this picture of the church? What do you find challenging?

6. What are some of the divisions that you see in our world between people that need to be healed? How do these worldly divisions make unity in diversity challenging for us in the church?

7. Which of these divisions has, personally, been difficult to overcome?

8. What benefits come from pursuing diversity as a church? How might we learn to see diversity as an asset rather than just a barrier to overcome? For some ideas, look at *1 Corinthians 12:12–28.*

9. What would it look like for your small group to be a place where people from a variety of backgrounds can learn from, appreciate, and encourage one another? Maybe draft up a list of "family rules" for your small group that would serve as the groundwork for ensuring that there is "no division in the body, but that its parts should have equal concern for each other." (1 Corinthians 12:25)

## Plan

During the *Plan* portion of your study you will be encouraged to make a conscious plan to apply God's Word to your daily life based on this study.

So break into pairs or triads and share the following:

- What part of the passage did you find most challenging? What do you think God is saying to you personally as a result of this study?

- How can you, specifically, respond to what God is saying? Some questions to help you process this are...

  - Is there a relationship that you realize that you need to work on this week?

  - Are there unconfessed biases that you realize have been keeping you from forming friendships with people in your own life? In the church?

Once you have all had a chance to share, talk about how you can hold each other accountable to the commitments God has called you to make this week. Maybe it involves sending each other a text message with how you have applied the passage in your life or offering to call each other up to pray about your personal applications. Whatever you decide, make it concrete and commit to follow up with each other at a specific time.

Conclude your time of sharing in prayer for one another.

## Conclusion

Conclude your group time by coming back together as a group and reminding one another to take some time in the daily devotions during the week.

Note that this **Apart** time is just as important as the **Together** portion of your study, as it is the place where you will continue to apply
what you have learned in your daily life.

Wrap up with any important group announcements before concluding your group time.

# Week One Devotions
## Unity in Diversity

---

## Day One: A Global Plan

*Then God said, "Let us make man in our image, after our*
*likeness. And let them have dominion over the fish of the sea*
*and over the birds of the heavens and over the livestock and*
*over all the earth and over every creeping thing that creeps on*
*the earth." So God created man in his own image, in the image*
*of God he created him; male and female he created them. And*
*God blessed them. And God said to them, "Be fruitful and*
*multiply and fill the earth and subdue it, and have dominion*
*over the fish of the sea and over the birds of the heavens and*
*over every living thing that moves on the earth."*
*~Genesis 1:26–28 (ESV)*

One couple in the Garden of Eden was never the ultimate plan. It
was just the beginning.

From the very start God's desire was that the human family would
fill the whole of creation; that we would stretch across continents
and traverse seas.

And as we did so we would become more diverse. Though all
made in the image of God, our different experiences and personalities would blossom into different cultures and ways of life. Though
one family, it would be a family made up of countless brothers and
sisters from radically different backgrounds.

St. Paul, when addressing the philosophers of Athens put it well when he said, "And he made from one man every nation of mankind to live on all the face of the earth, having determined allotted periods and the boundaries of their dwelling place." (Acts 17:26 ESV)

Put simply, God loves diversity within His family. It is something to be celebrated.

## Questions to Ponder

When was the last time you found yourself in a different community than your own? What was that experience like? How did that encounter of "difference" actually open your eyes to the beauty of another culture?

## Prayer

*Lord, thank you for placing me in a diverse world. Help me to appreciate, love, and give thanks for the different people around me, knowing that each one of them is made in your image. Amen.*

# Day Two: The Scope of Our Mission

*Jesus came to them and said, "All authority in heaven and on earth has been given to me. Therefore go and make disciples of all nations, baptizing them in the name of the Father and of the Son and of the Holy Spirit, and teaching them to obey everything I have commanded you. And surely I am with you always, to the very end of the age."*
*~Matthew 28:18–20 (NIV)*

The Great Commission never ceases to amaze me. Think about the scene for just a moment. Jesus is alive. He has risen from the dead and now stands before his ragtag group of disciples. Some are educated, others unschooled. Some had wealth while others were day laborers. All of them were Jewish and had spent the majority of their lives living in a geographical area only slightly larger than the state of New Jersey.

And now Jesus tells them that they are being called to go and preach the Good News of salvation to people from every nation. It must have seemed like a tall order for a couple of "everyday Joes" from Judea.

But what is amazing is they did it! Just a cursory glance at the book of Acts highlights the fact that these disciples went throughout the Roman world with the message about Jesus. But it becomes even more amazing when you consider the testimony of the early church. What they tell us is that these men traveled to such far-flung places as Ethiopia and India in their effort to make disciples. They were willing to cross geographical, ethnic, linguistic, and cultural boundaries for the sake of helping other people hear the message of Jesus Christ.

They entered a diverse world for the sake of sharing a message everyone needed to hear. They knew that everyone was in need of salvation and God had called them to be "ambassadors for Christ, God making his appeal through us." (2 Corinthians 5:20 ESV)

And so they went into new communities, entered new cultures, and became friends with people from every nation they encountered all for the sake of showing them the love of God in Christ.

## Question to Ponder

What boundaries exist between different groups of people in the community where you live? How does knowing that God loves them and desires to reach them encourage you to reach out and cross boundaries for the sake of sharing the Gospel?

## Prayer

> *Lord, too often I am intimidated by the diverse world around me. Help me to go wherever you send me for the sake of reaching the people that you long to reach with the Good News of Jesus Christ. Amen.*

# Day Three: The Source of Our Unity

*There is one body and one Spirit, just as you were called*
*to one hope when you were called; one Lord, one faith,*
*one baptism; one God and Father of all, who is over all*
*and through all and in all.*
*~Ephesians 4:4–6 (NIV)*

*"My prayer is not for them alone. I pray also for those*
*who will believe in me through their message, that all of them*
*may be one, Father, just as you are in me and I am in you.*
*May they also be in us so that the world may believe*
*that you have sent me."*
*~John 17:20–21 (NIV)*

Let's be honest, diversity is a major buzzword in our world today. Colleges, businesses, and even churches all laud diversity as something worth valuing and pursuing. And this makes sense! After all, we've already seen that God both loves diversity and desires people of every background to become a part of His family, the church.

But it naturally raises a question: "So what unites us?"

Too often our world settles for a kind of unity that is more about uniformity and promotes a kind of oneness that ignores differences for the sake of "not rocking the boat."

But God desires a kind of unity that is far deeper and more beautiful. It is a unity that springs from our connection with Him. In Ephesians, Paul says that our unity springs from the fact that we have all received the same grace from the same God. Likewise, the Holy Spirit works within us to make us one body, one family sharing a common faith.

This kind of unity allows for dynamic harmony in which we use our various gifts for common ends. It is a kind of unity that allows us to discuss and debate, even while pursuing common goals and a common mission. It gives us focus and holds us together as we bring our different gifts, personalities, backgrounds, and cultural sensibilities to the common table of the family of God, while also facing and overcoming the barriers that would otherwise separate us.

This is why Jesus' parting prayer for His disciples was so focused on unity. It is because He knew that this kind of unity is winsome, powerful, and points to the truth that we are all, indeed, one body in Christ.

## Question to Ponder

How is Christian unity different from the various other kinds of unity that we see in the world around us? How does this shape your own view of what it means to be united as the church?

## Prayer

*Lord, because of Jesus Christ you have made all Christians one family. Help me to remember this the next time I find myself in a disagreement with a brother or sister in Christ, and help us all to keep You and Your grace front and center in our lives so that we can, in all things, remain united for the sake of the mission You have given us. Amen.*

# Day Four: Delighting in Our Diversity

*Just as a body, though one, has many parts,*
*but all its many parts form one body, so it is with Christ.*
*For we were all baptized by one Spirit so as to form one*
*body—whether Jews or Gentiles, slave or free—and we were*
*all given the one Spirit to drink. Even so the body is not made*
*up of one part but of many... But in fact God has placed the*
*parts in the body, every one of them, just as he wanted them*
*to be. If they were all one part, where would the body be?*
*As it is, there are many parts, but one body.*
*~1 Corinthians 12:12–14 & 18–20 (NIV)*

Every so often you have a conversation that shapes the way that you think about your world. For me, that conversation came two weeks into my time with the UIC Gospel Choir. I joined the choir because one of my students encouraged me to start building more bridges between our college ministry and the black community on campus. She was a member of the choir and said it was a good place to start.

The conversation came when I sat down with one of the leaders of the choir to talk about the music we were singing. Coming from a predominantly white denomination where hymns were the standard fair in worship I was curious as to the influences and form of Gospel music.

"Why do we sing the same line over and over again?" I asked. He leaned back and thought a moment, and then shared the following: "In our community there isn't always a lot to celebrate. Most of us come from broken homes. We have people in our choir who've lost friends and family to violence. We need things that remind us of the hope we have. Gospel music is one of those things. Every time we sing a line of praise, it goes a little deeper into our bones. It goes a little deeper into our souls. We sing over and over again until the praises of God heal the hurts of our hearts and remind us of the greater hope we have."

With those words my friend opened my eyes to a richer reality of what it means to be a Christian in the world. He gifted me with a glimpse into what life is like for him and showed me how praising God actually transforms his world. His experience of worship has shifted and shaped how I approach God in my own faith journey.

That is the power of diversity in the Christian family. When we bring our different gifts to the table of God, we are all enriched by it. Our diversity—whether due to culture, experience, or gifting—is something that enriches the whole community. Our unity is not uniformity. It is sharing one heart as we exercise a variety of gifts for the sake of the whole.

## Questions to Ponder

When was the last time you were blessed by another person using their gifts? How did their experiences and expertise broaden your understanding of who God is and what His mission is all about?

## Prayer

*Lord, thank you for making me a part of a diverse family. Help me to affirm, encourage, appreciate, learn from, and celebrate the gifts of my brothers and sisters in Christ.*

# Day Five: Preparing for Heaven

*After this I looked, and there before me was*
*a great multitude that no one could count, from every nation,*
*tribe, people and language, standing before the throne*
*and before the Lamb. They were wearing white robes*
*and were holding palm branches in their hands.*
*And they cried out in a loud voice: "Salvation belongs*
*to our God, who sits on the throne, and to the Lamb."*
*~Revelation 7:9–10 (NIV)*

What does heaven look like? Typically, we think of things like pearly gates and a glowing city. Maybe we have visions of angels and thrones.

But stop and think for a minute? Who is there? What do they look and sound like?

In Revelation 7:9–10 the apostle John gets a glimpse of heaven and what he sees and hears is astounding. He writes that before him was a "multitude that no one could count, from every nation, tribe, people, and language." But how does he know this?

Well, because he can see them. He sees that they have different skin colors. He hears them praising God in different languages. The heavenly community is one of beautiful diversity, in which people from every background come together and praise God.

Sadly, too few of our churches in the West reflect this heavenly picture. Martin Luther King Jr. once lamented, "it is appalling that the most segregated hour of Christian America is eleven o'clock on Sunday morning." We often gather with those who look like us to sing songs that we're all comfortable with in a language all our own.

But the call of the church is to grow more diverse and not less: to increasingly become the heavenly community we are destined to be. Embracing diversity as Christians is not just a political or social ideal. It's a reflection of who we are as God's people and who we will one day become.

This is why healing divisions between people groups must be a priority of the church, and why diversity must be one of the markers of Christian community. In doing so, we become more and more the family God has called us to be.

**Questions to Ponder**

So are you ready for heaven? In what ways are you intentionally pursuing relationships with those who are different than you? What would it practically mean to be a church that reflects the incredible diversity of heaven?

**Prayer**

> *Lord, you have called us to be a family made up of people from every tribe, tongue, and nation. But too often we fail in this calling, preferring instead the company of those who are "like us." Help us to increasingly become the people we are called to be by reflecting the diversity of your heavenly kingdom. In the name of Jesus Christ we pray. Amen.*

# Speaking the Truth in Love

*"Handle them carefully, for words have more power than atom bombs."*

~Pearl Strachan Hurd

---

## Introduction

Words have power. In fact, author and speaker Yehuda Berg once wrote:

*"Words are singularly the most powerful force available to humanity. We can choose to use this force constructively with words of encouragement, or destructively using words of despair."*

In this session we are going to talk about the power of words and the role they can have either in helping or hindering our walk with Christ.

But before we dive into our study, let's take a moment to share what God has been doing in our lives this past week.

---

## Share

Break back up into pairs or triads, maybe even going back to the groups you spent time in at the conclusion of your last session.

Take a few moments to share one or more of the following:

- How did you do acting on the "Plan" you developed last week? What did you learn about yourself and God through that experience?

- What was something that stood out from your devotional time? Why was that so meaningful? What difference has that made in your life this past week?

---

## Hear

In our *Hear* portion this week we are going to listen to several passages that highlight the importance that words play in helping us grow as disciples.

So, take a few seconds to just sit and be silent.

Then, have one person read the following passages:

**John 8:31–32   Ephesians 4:11–16   Colossians 3:12–17**

After the text has been read, just take another moment of silence and then play the **Session 2: Speaking the Truth in Love** video.

VIDEO NOTES (FILL IN THE BLANK)

Our _____ are far more _____ than we often imagine.

_____ words have power because _____ words have power.

In order to _____ as disciples, we need other people in our lives who will speak _____ in a _____.

A key ingredient of _____ involves being willing to be held _____ by _____.

Three key questions for accountability:

- "Am I saying this in order to help this person _____?"

- "Is what I'm saying helping them become _____ or not?"

- "Does _____ I'm saying what I'm saying _____ Christlike _____?"

Give them the _____ of the _____ and assume that what they are saying is, ultimately, for your

_____.

---

## Explore

Let's take a closer look at each one of those passages in turn.

*John 8:31–32*

1. Jesus says, "If you hold to my teaching, you are really my disciples." What does it mean to "hold" to his teaching?

2. Why would Jesus make this one of the central marks of discipleship? What does he say are the benefits of holding to his teaching?

*Ephesians 4:11–16*

3. According to Paul, what is the goal of speaking the truth in love?

4. Why do you think he puts truth and love side by side here? What happens if you have one without the other?

*Colossians 3:12–17*

5. What virtues and attitudes should characterize Christian relationships with one another based on this passage?

6. What role do words play in this?

7. Why do you think Paul places forgiveness right in the middle of this passage? What role does forgiveness play in "teaching and admonishing one another"?

8. Paul begins and ends this text with a focus on Jesus. How does setting our sights on Him and giving thanks to Him help shape our relationships with one another?

## Apply

These three texts all focus on the power of words in the Christian life. At the heart of them is that passage from Ephesians 4:15:

*"Instead, speaking the truth in love, we will grow to become in every respect the mature body of him who is the head, that is, Christ."*

What Paul is highlighting is that an essential part of our discipleship is the giving and receiving of honest feedback and accountability, all in a spirit of love.

So let's take some time to reflect on this in our own lives.

9. Which side of the spectrum do you tend to fall on: truth or love? Why do you think that is? What would it look like to cultivate the other side so that you are truly able to "speak the truth in love"?

10. Think about the last time you received honest and loving feedback. How well did you handle it? If it was difficult, why was that? Are you more comfortable giving or receiving honest feedback?

11. What are the benefits of having others hold you accountable to your growth as a follower of Jesus? What are the benefits of having to hold *others* accountable to their growth as disciples?

12. What does it look like to speak the truth in love as a small group? How will you "let the message of Christ dwell in your

richly as you teach and admonish one another" during your times together?

## Plan

Break up into pairs or triads again. Try to partner up with different people from last time. Share one of the following:

- Which of these passages did you find most challenging? Why?
- What do you think God is saying to you personally as a result of this study?
- How can you, specifically, respond to what He is saying?

Try to be as specific as possible in terms of how you are going to put this study into practice during the week.

Once you have all had a chance to share, talk about how you can hold each other accountable to the commitments God has called you to make this week. Again, this can include text messages, phone calls for prayer, or even getting together outside of group for a cup of coffee to share what you are continuing to learn throughout the week.

Conclude your time of sharing in prayer for one another.

## Conclusion

Wrap up by coming back together as a group. Close with a prayer for your whole community, that you would be a small group that demonstrates what it means to speak the truth in love.

As always, don't forget to do the devotions during the week and come back ready to share what God has been up to during your time apart.

# Week Two Devotions
## Speaking the Truth in Love

---

## Day One: The Power of Words

*In the beginning God created the heavens and the earth.*
*Now the earth was formless and empty, darkness was over the*
*surface of the deep, and the Spirit of God was hovering over*
*the waters. And God said, "Let there be light," and there was*
*light...God saw all that he had made, and it was very good.*
*~Genesis 1:1–3 & 31*

Words have power. Many of us can vividly remember a harsh word spoken, the wounds of which are still in the process of healing. Likewise, we are comforted by the kinds words which brought encouragement in times of need. The idea that our words do not matter is, quite simply, untrue.

Words have power because that is how God made the world. When we look at the creation account in Genesis, what it so incredible is that God brings everything into being simply by speaking. And we, being made in his image, are also given the gift of speech; speech which can either be creative or destructive. Our words can build up or tear down. They can create new friends or ignite the sparks of animosity.

Proverbs says the following about the power of words: "The sooth-ing tongue is a tree of life, but a perverse tongue crushes the spirit" (Proverbs 15:4). This is why we need to carefully consider our words, for they are not neutral things. While our words cannot create in the same way God's words do, they do have the power to shape the world around us both in terms of the people they affect and the actions which result.

## Questions to Ponder

When was the last time you considered your words? When have you seen the power of words used—either for good or ill—in your life or the life of another person?

## Prayer

*Lord, too often I do not consider the power of my words. Help me to use them well, carefully considering the effect they have on others. May my words bring life to those I meet today. Amen.*

# Day Two: The Gift of Truth

*An honest answer is like a kiss on the lips...Better is open*
*rebuke than hidden love. Faithful are the wounds of a friend,*
*profuse are the kisses of an enemy.*
*~Proverbs 24:26 & 27:5–6*

Sometimes it can be difficult to tell other people the truth, especially when we know that it will be a truth that is difficult to hear. Knowing the power of words, it is easy to shy away from saying the right thing because we know that it has the potential to hurt those we love.

And yet, Scripture highlights the fact that speaking the truth is also a blessing that we desperately need. By telling people the truth, we give them an opportunity to grow and thrive. We can help highlight blind spots and address weaknesses that would otherwise continue to plague those around us.

Tim Keller writes that one of the marks of good words is that they are truthful, and that the failure to speak the truth to those who need to hear it is "fundamentally a lack of love." (*God's Wisdom for Navigating Life* by Tim & Kathy Keller. New York: Viking, 2017, p. 178).

This is why the writer of Proverbs says that "an honest answer is like a kiss on the lips...faithful are the wounds of a friend." Our friends are those who speak the truth to us with a desire to build us up and help us grow, even if initially hearing the truth stings.

### Questions to Ponder
When was the last time someone spoke the "loving truth" to you? How did you react? What does it look like to tell the truth in a way that builds up rather than burns down?

**Prayer**

*Lord Jesus, you call us to be people who speak the truth in love. Give me the courage to be lovingly honest with the people you have placed in my life, so that they may grow to be more and more like you. Amen.*

# Day Three: Speaking with Kindness and Gentleness

> *Anxiety weighs down the heart, but a kind word cheers it up...A gentle answer turns away wrath, but a harsh word stirs up anger.*
> ~Proverbs 12:25 & 15:1

"Honesty is the best policy." Growing up this was a pretty popular phrase. But it is also a phrase that has been abused of late. Too often I have heard people speak harsh words of truth to one another followed by the phrase, "I'm sorry, but I'm just being honest." Honesty is indeed the best policy, but only when tempered with kindness and gentleness.

You see, speaking the truth is important because it considers the content of our words. But we also need to consider the intention behind our words as well as the form that those words take.

This is where kindness and gentleness come in.

Kindness forces us to ask the question, "Why am I telling the truth to this person? Is it to win an argument? Undermine something they've said? Defend my pride? OR am I speaking the truth for his or her benefit? It is to really encourage, build up, and support this person?"

Likewise, gentleness challenges us to consider the tone and demeanor of our words. This kind of gentleness does not necessarily mean we always agree with the other person, but it ensures that what we say is communicated in a respectful way that de-escalates tense interactions.

One commentator writes, "Harsh words play well with people who already agree with you, but they won't persuade or help the truth to spread. Follow the one who, when he was reviled, did not revile in return." (1 Peter 2:23) (*God's Wisdom for Navigating Life* by Tim and Kathy Keller, New York: Viking 2017, p. 185.)

## Questions to Ponder

How well do you do in speaking the truth with kindness and gentleness? What might need to change in your motives and your demeanor when entering into honest conversations with others?

## Prayer

*Lord, you always used words that balanced truth, kindness, and gentleness. Teach me to speak boldly, but in ways that are heard, and honestly, but in ways that communicate kindness and respect. Amen.*

# Day Four: Rotten Talk

*Let no corrupting talk come out of your mouths,*
*but only such as is good for building up, as fits the occasion,*
*that it may give grace to those who hear.*
*~Ephesians 4:29*

Nothing is more destructive to a community than gossip. It sows the seeds of mistrust, discord, and anger. Proverbs actually says, "With their mouths the godless destroy their neighbors." (Proverbs 11:9)

In writing to the church at Ephesus, the apostle Paul warns, "Let no corrupting talk come out of your mouths." The word here literally means "rotten or spoiled" talk. It was a term used to describe food that had gone bad; stuff that isn't worth consuming because of how sickening it is.

Yet too often churches can be breeding grounds for gossip. Rather than talking face-to-face with the person with whom we have a disagreement or concern, we tell everyone else about our suspicions and frustrations. But such behavior is corrosive, destructive, and rotten.

But such behavior is not what is acceptable in the household of God. Paul tells us to only speak what is for the building up of another. Likewise, Jesus says, "If your brother sins against you, go and tell him his fault, between you and him alone. But if he does not listen, take one or two others along with you, that every charge may be established by the evidence of two or three witnesses. If he refuses to listen to them, tell it to the church" (Matthew 18:15–16). How often, though, do we get that backwards, going to others before we ever approach our brother or sister in faith?

The encouragement here is to resolve your disputes directly, lovingly, and with an aim to encourage and build one another up. Such talk is both lifegiving and a faithful witness to the love that we have for one another in Christ.

## Questions to Ponder

When you have a conflict with someone, what is your knee jerk reaction? Is it to go directly to the person or to go to others? How might your relationships with people change if you were to follow both Paul's and Jesus' advice?

## Prayer

*Lord, help me to avoid gossip and godless chatter. By Your Holy Spirit, make me into a peacemaker whose words give grace and are used for the sake of building up the body of Christ.*

# Day Five: God's Words to You

*And the Word became flesh and dwelt among us,*
*and we have seen his glory, glory as of the only Son*
*from the Father, full of grace and truth...*
*[Jesus said] "If you remain in me and my words remain*
*in you, ask whatever you wish, and it will be done for you.*
*This is to my Father's glory, that you bear much fruit,*
*showing yourselves to be my disciples. "As the Father has*
*loved me, so have I loved you. Now remain in my love.*
*If you keep my commands, you will remain in my love, just as*
*I have kept my Father's commands and remain in his love.*
*I have told you this so that my joy may be in you and*
*that your joy may be complete. My command is this:*
*Love each other as I have loved you."*
*~John 1:14 (ESV) & John 15:7–12 (NIV)*

How does God use His words with us? The interesting answer that John gives in his gospel is that God's Word comes to us to be with us. God's greatest Word to us is His Son, Jesus, who came with both grace and truth to save His wayward people. Though we had turned our backs on Him, cursed Him, and shunned Him, He pursued us with words of grace and truth.

Furthermore, Jesus says that His own example is supposed to shape how we interact with one another as well. On the night He was betrayed He told His disciples to abide in His word, keep His commandments, and love one another as He has loved them. And those words of encouragement are meant to be words of encouragement to us as well.

To speak the truth in love is to act in a way that points people to Jesus, the One who is full of grace and truth. In how we speak and interact with others we are to become signposts pointing others to God.

**Questions to Ponder**

How does reflecting on Jesus' example shape how you think about speaking the truth in love? Do your words show the world what it means to look, live, and love more like Jesus?

**Prayer**

*Lord God, I thank you that you speak words of grace and truth to me. I praise you that the greatest Word you spoke to me was through Your Son Jesus Christ, who came to forgive me, save me, and set me free. By Your Holy Spirit, help me always to speak the truth in love so that each person I meet may know the love, grace, and truth that only You can give. Amen.*

# Test Your Faith

*"Courage is not simply one of the virtues,*
*but the form of every virtue at the testing point."*

~C.S. Lewis

*"Testing leads to failure,*
*and failure leads to understanding."*

~Burt Rutan

## Introduction

You've made it to week three in our study together! As we have studied the importance of becoming disciples that make disciples, so far we have learned that growth happens best in a diverse community dedicated to helping one another grow. And we've learned the importance of speaking the truth in love in that community.

This week we turn our attention to another important discipleship topic—the need to test our faith. The Apostle Paul wrote:

*"Examine yourselves to see whether you are in the*
*faith; test yourselves. Do you not realize that Christ*
*Jesus is in you—unless, of course, you fail the test?"*

~2 Corinthians 13:5

Tests can be frightening things. "Test anxiety" is a reality for many people! Add to this the idea the fact that Paul warns us that failing the test can put our relationship with Jesus in question, and the stakes are high!

42

But we will find this week that testing is an important part of growth. God does not want you to fail! In fact, he knows that through examining our faith in the community of our Christian family, we can grow more and more like Jesus and become the disciples he created us to be.

## Share

Get back together with the pair or triad you planned with last week. Spend some time together on the following questions:

- Which way did the pendulum swing in your interactions with others this week? Was it more toward "truth" or more toward "love?"

- Is there a specific interaction with someone from this past week you wish you could do over again? What would you do differently?

- How did you seek to personally put last week's lesson into practice? How did that go?

Once you've had a chance to share, take a moment to pray for your time together this evening.

## Hear

During the *Hear* portion of your group time this week we will explore a number of places in the Bible that deal with testing our faith, and what it means to have weaknesses and strengths on our discipleship journey.

First, take a few seconds to just sit and be silent.

Then, have one person read the following passage:

### *2 Corinthians 13:1–6*

After the text has been read, just take another moment of silence and then play the *Session 3: Test Your Faith* video.

VIDEO NOTES (FILL IN THE BLANK)

_____ and _____ are important if we are to grow in our faith.

There are two "sides" to our faith. One comes _____ and the other comes _____ as we live out our faith.

Both _____ and _____ are _____ .

We _____ God as we gather on the weekends and in our personal devotional time.

We _____ with other believers in small groups and in other relationships, living out God's command to love one another.

We _____ by using our talents to make a difference in our church family and in the world around us.

We _____ our faith with those who need to know about the hope we have through Jesus.

We _____ at least one other person as together we seek to be disciples who make disciples.

We are _____ with the resources God has given us, and

We are willing to be held _____ as we encourage one another to remain faithful and continue to grow.

Weaknesses are opportunities for me to _____ .

Sometimes I am _____ to my own weaknesses.

_____

## Explore

In the *Explore* section we are going to take a closer look at our theme passage itself in order to discover what it means to those who wrote and originally heard it.

Read John 6:1–14. You've probably heard this story before, but there is a detail that we want to explore together.

1. We are told in v. 5 that Jesus sees the large crowd, and recognizes it is a "teachable moment" for his disciples. Note the question Jesus asks Philip. Why did he ask this question?


2. Jesus knows the impossibility of the situation, but also knows he has the power to overcome the impossible. What was Jesus hoping Philip would say to his question? What grade would you give Philip's response?

3. Andrew has a different answer, maybe getting closer to what Jesus was hoping to hear. What is good in Andrew's answer? What did he still need to learn?

4. When they see Jesus feed the 5000, what lesson do they learn?

5. Years later, Paul encouraged the Corinthian church to test their faith as well. Read 2 Corinthians 13:4–5. What does Paul say is the solution to the unresolved sin in their lives? How would testing their faith help give them access to this power?

## Apply

In the *Apply* section we are going to get a bit more personal as we consider the implications that this text has for our own lives.

6. During the video you were encouraged to think about our seven values and do a little "self-testing" of your own. Take a minute to give yourself a "grade" (A, B, C, D, or F) in each value right now.

_____ Worship (weekly together and personal time with God)

_____ Connect (in a small group and participating fully there)

_____ Serve (using your gifts to serve Trinity and the community)

_____ Share (relationships with those far from God in which you witness your faith)

_____ Lead (a willingness and chance to focus on the growth of at least one other person)

_____ Generosity (responding to the needs of others and tithing to your church family)

_____ Accountable (comfortable and willing to share how you are doing!)

7. Share with your group: What questions do you have with the values? Which is your best area? Your weakest? Where would you like to grow the most right now? Where do you feel stuck?

8. Share a time with your group when you saw God faithfully help you grow as a disciple. What scripture was helpful? Who did God use to help you test yourself and grow?

---

## Plan

During the *Plan* portion of your study you will again be encouraged to make a conscious plan to apply God's Word to your daily life based on this study.

So break into pairs or triads and share the following:

- What do you think God is saying to you personally as a result of this study?

- What one, concrete growth step could you take this week…

  - That responds to the area of growth you named above?
  - That someone could ask you about next week as a way of helping you take that step of growth and faith?

One tool that Trinity provides for group leaders and group members to help them "examine themselves" and "test your faith" is the Spiritual Life Assessment. Discuss the possibility of taking this online assessment and finding a time with your group leader or another member of the group to go deeper into your possible areas of strength and weakness. Your group leader can provide you with the online link and further instructions, and can help you get "paired up" to go over your results.

Conclude your time of sharing in prayer for one another.

## Conclusion

Conclude your group time by coming back together as a group and reminding one another to take some time in the daily devotions during the week. Encourage one another in this process of life-long evaluation and growth!

Note that this **Apart** time is just as important as the **Together** portion of your study, as it is the place where you will continue to apply what you have learned in your daily life.

Wrap up with any important group announcements before concluding your group time.

# Week Three Devotions

---

## Day One: Twins!

*"And it was He who gave some to be apostles, some to be prophets, some to be evangelists, and some to be pastors and teachers, to equip the saints for works of ministry, to build up the body of Christ, until we all reach unity in the faith and in the knowledge of the Son of God, as we mature to the full measure of the stature of Christ."*
*~Ephesians 4:11–13*

John gives us an interesting detail about the disciple Thomas that none of the other Gospels reveal. In John 11:16 we read, "So Thomas, called Didymus, said to the other disciples…" The word "didymus" means "repeat" or "double." Or, as most scholars suggest for this verse, "twin." So why was Thomas called "the twin"? Many scholars believe the explanation is simple. He looked like Jesus.

If that is true, imagine the confusion. How often did someone come up to Thomas expecting to have a conversation with Jesus? Did the other disciples tease him because he looked so much like their teacher and friend? Worst of all, was Thomas worried that the religious leaders, in their attempts to arrest or silence Jesus, might just mistakenly arrest him? In John 11, where we are first told Thomas was called "the Twin," Jesus has just decided to head back to Jerusalem. It is Thomas who tells the other disciples, "Let's go die with him."

Ephesians tells us that our goal is to all join Thomas in being called "the Twin." Our goal is to become like Jesus. We are to become mature in our faith, until we attain "the full measure of the stature of Christ." One translation says it this way, "We must become like a mature person, growing until we become like Christ." Of course, this does not mean we are to play dress up and try to physically resemble Jesus. It means we are to love the way he loved. To disciple others the way he discipled them. To care for others the way he cared for them. Our job is to live the way he lived.

The journey to become more like Jesus will never end until we are in heaven. Some days we will resemble him more than others. Every day we will rely on his grace and forgiveness for the moments when we fail. But we all look forward to the day we get called "the Twin" just like Thomas did!

**Question to Ponder**

What characteristic of Jesus can you ask God to help you see more of in yourself today?

**Prayer**

*Dearest Jesus, make me more like you every day. Amen.*

# Day Two: Truth and Love

*"Speaking the truth with love, we will grow up in every way into Christ, who is the head."*
~Ephesians 4:15

One year I had a student in my classroom that lied constantly. Every missed assignment was accompanied by a new excuse. His classmates grew sick of his stories designed to make him sound more talented and interesting than he really was. Any attempt on my part to help him learn from his mistakes was met with a refusal to accept he had made a mistake in the first place. There was always a reason why he was right or at least was not at fault.

The crazy thing was… I kind of liked the kid. He was funny and engaging. I knew his home situation had been tough. He did have some amazing gifts, if you could see past the lies. I prayed that God would help me find a way to help him deal with his faults and become the person I knew God had made him to be.

Slowly, an amazing thing began to happen. He started to be more honest with me. He started to "own up" to his mistakes. To admit his failings. I was thankful that it appeared God was answering my prayer, although I wasn't really sure what had made the difference. Near the end of the school year, his mother and I were discussing the change we had seen. We both believed he was maturing, and that was a big help. But she also believed there was another important factor. "He sensed that you liked him. That you cared. And if you liked him, then maybe it was easier for him to like himself."

"Testing our faith" can be a scary proposition. Being open and honest with ourselves when it comes to our weaknesses and areas for growth can be tough. It gets worse if we have to be open and honest with someone else as well! Does God really intend for me to pay attention to my weaknesses, and let someone else see them? Do I really need to do that to grow more like Jesus?

Paul said it best. "Speaking the truth with love, we will grow up..." Truth and love must come together. Truth by itself is hard to hear. Love alone overlooks the truth I need. But truth, shared in an environment of love, makes all the difference. If I know I am loved, I can be truthful with the God that loves me! If I know others care, I can open up and let them see and share truth with me. Growth happens when I am willing to face the truth. I am willing to face the truth when I know I am loved.

## Question to Ponder

Who is the best person to share God's love and truth with you right now?

## Prayer

*Dear God, assure me that I am loved, so I can face the truth I need to hear and grow.*

# Day Three: Testing Can Be Tough

*"Consider it pure joy, my brothers and sisters,*
*whenever you face trials of many kinds, because you know*
*that the testing of your faith produces perseverance.*
*Let perseverance finish its work so that you may be mature*
*and complete, not lacking anything."*
~James 1:2–4

The doctor's words made me a little nervous. "I want you to have a stress test." I had no idea what that was, so I asked him what the test would entail. He explained they would hook me up to a machine that would monitor my heart. I would then get on a treadmill and they would keep making me go faster and faster on the treadmill until I couldn't go any faster or until my heart showed signs it was having an issue. Now I was more than a little nervous...

The test ended up being easier than I expected. The nurse assured me that they would stop whenever I needed to quit, and that they would warn me before they increased the speed of the treadmill. As the test went on, I found myself relaxing and almost enjoying the workout. And it turns out the test was very important. It revealed that my heart, under stress, was showing that there was something wrong. Further tests revealed a blockage that needed attention. The same doctor that ordered the stress test used a stent to fix the blockage, and the problem was solved. What an amazing miracle!

James warns us that trials will be a part of the life of a believer. These trials become tests of our faith. But God in His grace promises to use these trials to produce in us perseverance, and through that perseverance to bring about growth and maturity.

One of my former pastors used to say, "God never wastes a stressful time in your life." In other words, we can trust that the stresses of everyday life will be used by God to help us grow. Tests will come... but by God's grace the end result is we will find ourselves "not lacking anything!"

## Questions to Ponder

What stress are you encountering in life today? How is God using that stress to help you test your faith and grow?

## Prayer

*Heavenly Father, when I am in the middle of a time of testing and stress, help me to trust in you and look for your hand helping me to grow. Amen.*

# Day Four: Face Your Weaknesses

*"Purge me with hyssop, and I shall be clean; wash me,*
*and I shall be whiter than snow. Let me hear joy and gladness;*
*let the bones that you have broken rejoice. Hide your face from*
*my sins, and blot out all my iniquities. Create in me a clean*
*heart, O God, and renew a right spirit within me."*
~Psalm 51:7–10

In Tiger Woods' best season as a professional golfer he won 9 of 20 tournaments entered, including three major tournaments. That year, Tiger ranked first in scoring average, second in driving distance, second in putting, and first in the greens reached in the "regulation" number of strokes. He dominated almost every important statistical category except one: saving par when coming out of a sand trap. His "sand save" rank was 51st!

You might think Tiger spent a huge amount of time working on his sand game that off season. But he didn't. When asked about how he dealt with his relatively poor sand play his response was simple. "I try and make sure I don't hit the ball in the sand."

As Christians it is tempting to try and ignore our weaknesses. Rather than face them and fix them, we avoid the circumstances that might bring them to light and pretend that they are not there. The reason for this is clear: who wants to think about their weaknesses? I'd rather focus on my strengths. But weaknesses have a way of coming back to haunt us at just the wrong time. Under stress or in other difficult circumstances our weaknesses become liabilities and a place for us to be vulnerable to Satan's attacks. To grow more like Jesus we need to be willing to face our weaknesses.

King David was faced with a weakness. The prophet Nathan confronted him about a sin in his life. It would have been easy for David to gloss it over. He was, after all, the king, and one of the most powerful men in the world. But David acknowledged his sin. He confronted his weakness. He went to the Lord for forgiveness and grace. And he asked God for help. "Create in me a clean heart, O God..."

## Question to Ponder

What weakness or sin in your life can you place before God today, asking for his help to remove that weakness and help you grow?

## Prayer

*Dearest Jesus, search my heart and my life. Help me see where my weaknesses are keeping me from living the life you have for me. Amen.*

# Day Five: Setting an Example

*"Until I come, devote yourself to the public reading of*
*Scripture, to exhortation, to teaching...*

*Practice these things, immerse yourself in them,*
*so that all may see your progress."*
~1 Timothy 4:13,15

In the 1980's computers began to work their way into our everyday lives. "The Computer" was the 1983 Time Magazine "Machine of the Year." PC's began to show up on desks at work. The "home computer" became a useful tool instead of an excuse to play some games. But with these new modern marvels came occasional frustration. Waiting for the computer to complete a task could be maddening. You stared at a blank screen, not knowing if the computer was doing something or not. Would the program take one minute to load or ten? Was it successfully saving your database? Was anything happening inside that box?

Interface designer Bob Stahl wrote, "People wait for all sorts of things every day, sometimes more happily than others. The problem isn't the waiting... it's how the user feels about the waiting." About a year later a graduate student presented a paper about what he called "percent-done progress indicators," and the progress bar was born! The study found people were much happier waiting for a computer to complete a task if they could see that progress was being made. As long as the little bar kept getting bigger, people were less anxious. It didn't even matter if the bar was an accurate representation of the time left to complete the task!

Paul encouraged Timothy to study and teach the scriptures diligently. "Immerse yourself in them," he wrote, "so that all may see your progress." Notice that Paul is not only concerned with Timothy's growth, but he assumes that growth will be seen by others. This makes sense for a couple of reasons. First, other believers could hold Timothy accountable to grow. Timothy was a young pastor. He had a lot to learn! Knowing others expected that growth and were watching and encouraging him helped keep him on track. And that growth was also important as an inspiration for others. Seeing Timothy grow made it clear that growth was possible for all.

Many Christians have this "it's between me and God" mentality that can be dangerous to growth. Letting others see your growth and become aware of your progress is crucial. It keeps you on track. It encourages others. It's part of what it means to live in the family of God.

**Questions to Ponder**

Who is it that helps you monitor your growth? Who sees your progress as you grow more like Jesus?

**Prayer**

> *Holy Spirit, thank you for the gift of other believers in my life, to see my progress and encourage me to continue to grow. Amen.*

# Try and Discuss

*"God doesn't call people who are qualified. He calls people who are willing and then qualifies them."*
~Richard Parker

*"In most every business, you learn by doing. The apprenticeship model is much more effective than the classroom for cultivating entrepreneurs."*
~Andrew Yang

---

## Introduction

We have discovered in past weeks that an environment of diversity, honest conversations, and fearless self-evaluation creates a safe place for disciples to grow in their faith. While Jesus' disciples never received what we would think of as formal training, they became incredibly capable leaders in the early church. A key to their success was the way Jesus taught them to practice new behaviors. Jesus showed them what to do, discussed the "whys" of the teaching, and then he sent them out to do ministry without his direct involvement.

*And he called the twelve and began to send them out two by two...*
~Mark 6:7

This week we will learn how to replicate Jesus' hands on, try it out, talk about it way of teaching. Our goal is to first learn by being taught using Jesus' try and discuss method. As we experience

60

learning that compels us to put knowledge into action, we will also learn to use Jesus' method to teach others. Mastering Jesus' method of teaching is another important step in becoming a disciple that make disciples.

## Share

Get back together with the pair or triad you planned with last week. Spend some time together on the following questions:

What specific action steps did you take to address possible next steps of growth identified in the study last week?

If you took the online Spiritual Life Assessment, discuss your results. If you didn't take it, discuss why.

What challenges did you face as you were identifying your next steps?

Once you've had a chance to share, take a moment to pray for your time together today.

## Hear

During the *Hear* portion of your group time this week we will explore how Jesus taught disciples to disciple using the try and discuss model of learning.

First, take a few seconds to just sit and be silent.

Then, have one person read the following passages:

### Mark 6:7–13, 30–31

After the text has been read, just take another moment of silence and then play the **Session 4: Try and Discuss** video.

Jesus taught by challenging his disciples to move from

_____ and _____ to

_____ which results in life transformation,

not just the dispensing of information.

Jesus' hands-on method of teaching—the "_____ and

_____" method of learning!

Mark 3:15—"...**to be with him**"

"I am ready to, "_____" a person in an

_____ who will teach

me what I need to know and challenge me to practice the behav-

iors that Jesus wants to see in my life?"

In 1 Corinthians 11:1, the Apostle Paul says it this way: "Be

_____ of me, as I am of Christ."

Luke 8:21—Learning relationships are like family.

Jesus is saying to us today, "_____!" Every

disciple is called to learn how to look, live and love like Jesus so

that they can be sent to teach others to do the same.

Jesus method of teaching reproduced his knowledge and his behaviors in the lives of others—even when they were

_____ of themselves.

God's next step for my life is always one step outside of my

_____.

Jesus' "try and discuss" method of teaching:

- Demonstrate—I do. You watch. We talk.
- Involve—I do. You help. We talk.
- Assist—You do. I help. We talk.
- Observe—You do. I watch. We talk.
- Multiply—You do. Someone else watches. We talk.

Where do you need the "try and discuss" method of teaching in your life? Who could walk you through these five steps?

## Explore

In the *Explore* section we are going to take a closer look at Mark 6 in order to discover what it means to those who wrote and originally heard it.

1. In Mark chapter 4 through 6 read the headings in your Bible. What activities do you see Jesus doing?

2. Read Mark 3:14–15. What did Jesus do before he began all the ministry activities noted above?

3. Imagine the disciples watching Jesus as he taught about God's Kingdom and demonstrated its power by doing miracles. What range of emotions do you think the disciples experienced?

4. In Mark 6:7, Jesus gives the disciples their assignment. What does the disciple's assignment tell you about the Kingdom of God?

5. Jesus instructions in verse 8 at first glance might seem unwise. What will the disciples learn by following these instructions?

6. Verses 10 and 11 are a sobering warning that not everyone will accept the Kingdom of God. Why is the message of repentance rejected? What tensions do you think they felt about giving up on someone who has heard and rejected their message?

7. Jesus gave them the authority over evil in verse 7. In what ways did Jesus command them to use their authority in verse 12 and 13? What excuses might the disciples have offered when told to do these things?

8. What happens in Mark 6:30–31? What does Jesus encourage the disciples to do after their first hands-on ministry experience? What do you think they talked about while resting?

---

## Apply

In the *Apply* section we are going to get a bit more personal as we consider the implications that this text has for our own lives.

9. During the video and our *Explore* time we reviewed the "try and discuss" method of teaching that Jesus used to train his disciples to look, live and love like him. Here are the steps:

   • Demonstrate—I do. You watch. We talk.

   • Involve—I do. You help. We talk.

   • Assist—You do. I help. We talk.

   • Observe—You do. I watch. We talk.

   • Multiply—You do. Someone else watches. We talk.

   What advantages does this model of learning provide the learner and the teacher? What fear or anxiety might you experience if you were being taught using this model of learning?

10. Discuss the idea of ministering with Jesus' authority. What does that mean for you as you look, live, and love more like Jesus?

11. What growth steps do you believe God would like you to take today with the help of someone who would use the "try and discuss" method with you?

12. Trinity's goal is to raise up people in all small groups to help others take a next step in faith by providing encouragement, prayer, and training using the "try and discuss" method of learning. We call this role a "Discipler." What questions or concerns would you have about working with a Discipler to help you take your next step in faith? What characteristics and qualifications would be important for this person? Is there someone in your group that you might trust in this role?

## Plan

During the *Plan* portion of your study you will again be encouraged to make a conscious plan to apply God's Word to your daily life based on this study.

Break into pairs or triads and share the following:

- What do you think God is saying to you personally as a result of this study?

- What growth step could you take this week?

- Who could help teach you about this step using the try and discuss method?

Conclude your time of sharing in prayer for one another.

## Conclusion

Conclude your group time by coming back together and sharing some of your growth steps. It's possible that you might be able to join with others who are desiring to learn the same things you are. Set up a system of accountability throughout the week to remind each other to focus on the agreed on action steps in this lesson.

Remind one another to take some time in the daily devotions during the week. Staying in God's Word will strengthen you to carry out your next steps.

# Week Four Devotions

---

## Day One: Hungry?

*Train up a child in the way he should go;*
*even when he is old he will not depart from it.*
*~Proverbs 22:6 (ESV)*

We often hear this verse quoted when children go astray, and parents are praying for them to return. Here's another perspective on the verse. Consider that you are the child that has grown up. How were you trained as a child to follow Jesus? We need to recognize that not everyone had parents that did a great job communicating what it means to look, live and love more like Jesus. We can be grown, but still be very young in the faith, but that's okay! Whether you had a strong Christian upbringing or not, we are all called to a life-long commitment to learning God's word and practicing to be more like Jesus. Are you hungry for this kind of life?

The phrase "train up" in the original Hebrew language describes a midwife dipping her finger into crushed dates and then rubbing the palate of the mouth of a newborn child to stimulate the infant's desire for milk. To "train up" a child means to create a hunger within him or her for God's word which leads to living God's way. The word for "child" in this passage is used throughout the Bible to describe an infant, a young boy, Joseph at age 17, and a young man ready for marriage. No matter what age or stage we are in our lives, we need spiritual parents that arouse our appetite for the word of God. Ongoing sustenance of God's word throughout life is the only thing that will keep us from departing from Jesus' way.

The Apostle Paul writes on the problem of a shortage of spiritual parents in 1 Corinthians 4:15, "For though you have countless guides in Christ, you do not have many fathers. For I became your father in Christ Jesus through the gospel." Each of us needs a spiritual parent in our lives to continue to kindle our desire to know more of God's plan as revealed in his word and practice it every day. As we grow, we are called to inspire that longing in those who are younger in the faith than we are!

## Questions to Ponder

What stimulates a deeper hunger for God's word in your life? Who is helping to arouse that appetite in this season of your life? Is there someone you could "train up" so they would develop a stronger desire for learning the way of Jesus?

## Prayer

*Father, thank you for the gift of those who make us crave your word. Guide me and direct me to follow the way of Jesus every day of my life. As I grow, help me to be a spiritual parent to others that I might create a craving in others for your word. Amen.*

# Day Two: Growing Up

*For though by this time you ought to be teachers, you need*
*someone to teach you again the basic principles of the oracles*
*of God. You need milk, not solid food, for everyone who lives*
*on milk is unskilled in the word of righteousness, since he is*
*a child. But solid food is for the mature, for those who have*
*their powers of discernment trained by constant practice to*
*distinguish good from evil.*
*~Hebrews 5:12–14 (ESV)*

Did you have a growth chart at home as a child? Maybe it was inside the closet doorjamb to mark your height and the date. Every so often, your mom or dad would excitedly have you stand with your back against the jamb and mark your progress, marveling in the distance between the lines from the last measurement!

But what would your parents have done if you had stopped growing or even shrunk? They would have immediately taken you to the doctor to find out what was wrong! Our physical growth is a sign that indicates health. A failure to mature would be a cause for worry.

When it comes to our spiritual growth, sometimes we stop growing or even regress. The writer of Hebrews sounds the alarm. Apparently, the people he is addressing must be taught "again the basic principles." They had been maturing in the faith, but are now behaving like children who must return to spiritual milk! Just as a baby grows and needs solid food to develop, Christians need to be able to digest solid spiritual food to grow up into maturity.

This week in our small groups we are considering how Jesus taught his disciples to become mature followers. There is a critical difference between growing up physically and growing up spiritually. One happens without much effort, but the other required our participation or "constant practice" as our verse says. Jesus' way of teaching pushes us to choose to consume the solid food necessary to be more like him. We not only encounter his word; we are pushed to practice it. If our behaviors don't change, we stop growing and even begin "shrinking." The lack of spiritual growth over time is dangerous because it leaves us unable to distinguish good from evil and we will struggle to live out God's plan for our lives.

## Questions to Ponder

How would you describe your spiritual growth? What would a diet of spiritually "solid food" that strengthens you to move from knowing to doing look like? What barriers do you sense in your life that keep you from more fully practicing your faith?

## Prayer

*Lord, thank you for the solid food of your word that helps us to grow up. I pray today for someone who will teach me as Jesus taught his disciples by challenging me. Help me to not just know about faith, but push me to the constant practice of my faith that I would be able to distinguish good from evil and live as a maturing believer in Christ. Amen.*

# Day Three: Teach them to Obey

*Go therefore and make disciples of all nations, baptizing them in the name of the Father and of the Son and of the Holy Spirit, teaching them to observe all that I have commanded you. And behold, I am with you always, to the end of the age."*
*~Matthew 28:19–20 (ESV)*

Jesus' "final will and testament" for his disciples was to, "make disciples!" He goes on to say this is done by baptizing and teaching. In baptism God gives the gift of faith freely, not based on anything we do, but because of his love for us. But baptism is only the beginning of disciplemaking!

There are two occurrences of the word "all" in this passage meaning "every or whole." The first all points to the **breadth** of the assignment—God desires *all* people to be saved so we are to "make disciples of *all* nations." The second all points to the **depth** of the assignment, "...teach them to observe *all* that I have commanded." Failure to teach the depth results in a failure to reach the breadth. As we learned yesterday, it's solid food that moves us from knowing to doing. If we don't consume this solid food, we won't have the people and resources needed to reach all nations.

A recent study identified that only 42% of church goers spend time with other believers to teach them the faith. This means most Christians have a truncated view of the Great Commission, our verse for today. Ultimately, this results in adults who don't know how to live out their faith in ways that will make more disciples. Is teaching people to observe or live out what Jesus commanded a primary concern for you?

Many Christians wrongly believe they are not qualified to help others to grow in their faith. They attend Bible classes, read books and listen to sermons hoping one day they will know enough to teach others—but that day never comes. The only way to master this skill is to do it. You can't learn to swim in a classroom! What's your first step? First, you seek to find someone who can disciple you! As you grow, you can disciple others using what you have learned. It's in the teaching of the faith to others that our faith becomes stronger, more powerful, more real and more purposeful.

## Questions to Ponder

Do you have excuses as to why God couldn't use you to disciple someone else? Make a list and spend some time asking God to show you how to overcome your fears and take steps to help others grow in the faith.

## Prayer

*Father, we know through your Son, Jesus, that you desire all people to be saved. Please help me see that you want to use me. Give me the boldness needed to step up and get involved in the spiritual life of others. Open my eyes to see the opportunities to teach others everything you have commanded. Surround me with people who can support me in this role. I pray these things in Jesus' name, Amen!*

# Day Four: Have You Arrived?

*...God our Savior, who desires all people to be saved
and **to come** to the knowledge of the truth.*
~1 Timothy 2:4 (ESV)

*...burdened with sins and led astray by various passions,
always learning and never able **to arrive** at a knowledge
of the truth.*
~2 Timothy 3:7 (ESV)

Have you arrived? The question conjures up images of people celebrating material success, but there is a much more important destination! In our passages above we see two possible endpoints. Some people arrive at the knowledge of the truth, and others who are burdened with sin are led astray and never reach the truth. Where are you on this journey? Jesus helped his disciples come to the knowledge of the truth by teaching them the answers to these four questions:

Origins: Where did I come from?

Meaning: Why am I here?

Morality: How should I live?

Destiny: What happens after I die?

Your answers reveal your worldview, the lens through which you make decisions about everything in life. Have you ever updated a prescription for your glasses or contacts and been amazed at how clear everything looks? A biblical worldview brings clarity and relevance to your life as you align your thinking and acting with the knowledge of the truth. As we continue to grow as Christians, we need to have honest and open conversations about our worldview to keep us sharply focused on the knowledge of the truth that comes only from God.

In today's "all religion is true" world, much of the teaching about God confuses people and gives them the wrong answers. As a result, people are seeing a garbled view of life. They are being led away from the knowledge of the truth and sadly away from Jesus and his offer of forgiveness and eternal life.

Consider God's answers to these four questions by measuring them to all other possibilities. Don't be afraid to dig in and test God's answers in the Bible. He has provided responses that are logical, verifiable and don't contradict one another. Test all other worldviews, and you will find they don't measure up to these standards. Have you arrived at the knowledge of the truth?

**Questions to Ponder**

What are your answers to the four worldview questions? Here are four verses that might help: Genesis 1:1, Matthew 4:19, John 15:7 and John 11:25. What other answers have you considered? What arguments or questions keep you from Biblical worldview?

**Prayer**

> *Father, help me to arrive at the knowledge of the truth about you as I study the gift of your Son Jesus. Keep my thoughts about our world and your plan and purpose sharply in focus that I might live my life for your purpose and respond to this world with your love and grace given through Jesus, Amen!*

# Day Five: Follow Me!

*And he said to them, "Follow me,*
*and I will make you fishers of men.*
~Matthew 4:19 (ESV)


*Then Jesus told his disciples, "If anyone would come after me,*
*let him deny himself and take up his cross and follow me.*
~Matthew 16:24 (ESV)

Who are you following? The average number of friends people follow on Facebook is 338! On Facebook, you might find out about their likes and dislikes, their raves and rants, their kids, vacations, and hobbies—not to mention the funny animal videos! Thankfully, you have an option to block posts without offending a friend by unfriending them!

In our first verse from early in his ministry, Jesus calls the disciples to follow him into mission. Much later, in our second verse, he reveals the true nature of what this calls means. Following Jesus is more than casually checking a news feed! Jesus says it's about denial of self. At first, we might recoil at such an austere idea. But, imagine being content with your life. No more insisting on your own way, giving of unasked-for advice, trying to make a good impression, or manipulating circumstances to your advantage. What if you could leave behind the "I want, I have, and I do" self-focused life? Could your priority response in all things become a reflection Christ's love? Remember, Jesus would never ask us to do something that was out of reach.

The key is the Cross. Jesus says, "take up your cross and follow me." Some people make this into a burden in life that you must bear like a bad relationship or illness. But remember Jesus made this statement before he had to carry his Cross! He was foreshadowing his denial of self for our sake. Jesus is connecting our denial of self to his example. To follow Jesus, we must be willing to follow him to the Cross. Why? It's there we find the power to deny ourselves! At the Cross, we are reborn as new people, with his Spirit, and his power to live our lives following him.

Jesus says in the Matthew 16:25, "For whoever would save his life will lose it, but whoever loses his life for my sake will find it." Jesus promises real life from following him and turning away from self. All this begins with learning as we have studied this week - from milk to solid food, growing up into obedient disciples focused on the knowledge of the truth. Jesus is regularly "posting" his truth for your life. Are you paying as much attention to him as you are your Facebook feed? Remember, he is checking in on the details of our lives every minute and he will never unfriend us! Like if you agree!

**Question to Ponder**

How has your understanding of following Jesus grown during our small group study?

**Prayer**

*Lord Jesus Christ, as I hear Your call and face the challenge to follow you, give me the boldness to leave behind those things that would be a hindrance, and enable me to take up the challenge obediently. Amen.*

# Witness— Sharing Our Faith

*"I do not know anything that would wake up Chicago better than for every man and woman here who loves Him to begin to talk about Him to their friends, and just to tell them what He has done for you. You have got a circle of friends. Go and tell them of Him."*

~Dwight L. Moody

## Introduction

In this fifth week of our study, we will be encouraging one another to grow in our witness to others for Jesus. Often Christians are hesitant and even fearful of discussing this essential part of our faith, but we shouldn't let fear keep us from this topic! A witness provides evidence or testimony to convince others of the truth. As Christians, we are called to provide evidence of who Jesus is, what he has done for humanity, and what it means to follow him. Our witness foundational to every Christian's identity—it is not an optional activity of our faith. The question that we must ask ourselves is, "What does my life say to others about Jesus?"

While our witness begins with our behaviors, it doesn't end there. Maybe you have heard the quip, "Preach the Gospel at all times. Use words when necessary!" This statement highlights the importance of our behaviors, but it misses the point of the Gospel. Jesus is our model for behavior, "the Word made flesh." He spoke the truth about who God is, identifying the problem of sin and how his death and resurrection are the only solution to this problem that has the power to separate people from God forever. Our behavior and our words are both required to share this good news with others as Jesus instructed us in the Great Commission.

Jesus promises the Holy Spirit's presence and power in order for us to witness to the world.

> *But you will receive power when the Holy Spirit*
> *has come upon you, and you will be my witnesses*
> *in Jerusalem and in all Judea and Samaria,*
> *and to the end of the earth."*
> *~Acts 1:8*

Remember our mission statement is to look, live and love more like Jesus. The Holy Spirit's power will shape our behaviors, but he will also do for us what he has done for millions of Christians that have gone before us, he will help us give a verbal testimony of faith and the ability to speak when the right moment presents itself. Are you ready to experience the work of the Holy Spirit? You will sense his power and presence as you are a witness for Jesus!

---

## Share

Get back together with the pair or triad you planned with last week. Spend some time together on the following questions:

- What specific action steps did you take to address possible next steps of growth identified in the study last week?
- How was the "try and discuss" method used in your growth steps?
- What successes did you experience in your learning?
- What barriers did you face in using the "try and discuss" method to take a growth step?
- Who is helping you and holding you accountable in your growth?

Once you've had a chance to share, take a moment to pray for your time together today.

# Hear

During the *Hear* portion of your group time this week we will explore how Jesus sent his disciples into the world to be witnesses.

First, take a few seconds to just sit and be silent. Then, have one person read the following passages:

### Acts 1:1–11, 1 Peter 3:13–15

After the text has been read, take another moment of silence and then play the **Session 5: Witness—Sharing Our Faith** video.

VIDEO NOTES (FILL IN THE BLANK)

*Barna Survey—How would you respond?*
"I, personally, have a responsibility to tell other people about my religious beliefs."

_____% of Christians believe that personally sharing their

faith is important.

_____% of the people actually do share their faith with

someone else.

*Trinity's Share Challenge:*
Over the next six months, commit to share the Gospel of Jesus with two people who don't follow Jesus.

Our story helps us _____ and possibly even

_____ the answer to the question, "What has God

done for me through Jesus?"

God has saved us from an eternity in hell separated from God

through an astonishing act of _____.

The _____ in telling our story about what God

has done for us is to make sure we have _____!

Here are five actions you can take that will prepare the way for you
to be a blessing to others and open doors to sharing your story:

- B _____

- L _____

- E _____

- S _____

- S _____

## Explore

In the *Explore* section we are going to take a closer look at Acts
1:1–11 in order to discover what it means to those who wrote and
originally heard it.

1. What emotions do you think the disciple's experienced as Jesus
   left them?

2. Jesus offered "many proofs" that he was alive (v. 3) What proof
   have you needed to convince you that Jesus is alive?

3. Jesus commands them to "wait for the gift." What questions might you have asked regarding this gift? How have you experienced the Spirit as you have witnessed to others?

4. What does the disciples' question reveal about their lack of clarity about Jesus' mission? How has lack of clarity held you back from carrying out Jesus' mission?

5. Jesus says they will be his witnesses. Did the first disciples have an advantage over us in their ability to witness? Why or why not?

6. Jesus describes a huge mission as he sends the disciples to the end of the earth. What does this tell you about God's confidence in people to carry out his mission and the power of the Holy Spirit?

7. Examine I Peter 3:13–15. How does Peter explain his understanding of what it takes to be a witness after having the experience of living as a witness?

## Apply

In the *Apply* section we are going to get a bit more personal as we consider the implications that this text has for our lives.

8. What is your reaction to Jesus calling you to be a witness for him?

9. During the video, we discussed five ways to be a witness of Christ's love to others. Discuss your ideas for preparing for and practicing your witness as you:

- Begin with prayer for those you encounter
- Listen for how God is already working in their lives
- Engage people by "doing life" in social settings—meals, hobbies, events, children
- Serve people by giving yourself to help with physical, spiritual and emotional needs
- Share your faith story by telling how your life has changed as your story and God's story intersect.

How can your group encourage one another in these behaviors?

*Resources:*
- Engaging in Story—Connecting our story with THE Story—a tool to help you develop your story
- BlessEveryHome.com—a tool to help you connect with your neighbors

## Plan

During the *Plan* portion of your study you will again be encouraged to make a conscious plan to apply God's Word to your daily life based on this study.

Break into pairs or triads and share the following:

- What do you think God is saying to you personally as a result of this study?
- What one, concrete growth step could you take this week?

Conclude your time of sharing in prayer for one another and for those you believe God has placed in your life to reach with the good news of Jesus.

## Conclusion

Conclude your group time by coming back together as a group and reinforcing your commitment to set aside ample time to work on your planning growth steps. How can you hold one another accountable for the growth steps that were identified? Remember you will be asked to share with your group how you engaged in your growth steps. Your victories and the challenges and difficulties of these steps are both encouraging and instructive to others. Remember to take note of both to share next week.

Wrap up with any important group announcements before concluding your group time.

# Week Five Devotions

## Day One: B.L.E.S.S.—Begin with Prayer

*For the Son of Man came to seek and to save the lost.*
*~Luke 10:19*

*Brothers, my heart's desire and prayer to God for them*
*is that they may be saved.*
*~Romans 10:1 (ESV)*

Have you ever tried to share your faith with a non-Christian? Our attempts to share Jesus with others can be met with indifference, rejection or even anger. Try as we may, we don't experience the kind of connection that helps lost people receive Jesus as their Lord and Savior. But let's be honest, we are talking evangelism, right? At this point, most of us would like to excuse ourselves from the discussion! We can't if we want to be like Jesus who came to seek and save the lost. But how can we do the same?

Researcher Mark Russell studied 12 mission organizations. Six of those groups were founded with a focus on the missionary goal of converting lost people. He called those groups the "converters." The other six groups were focused on contributing to the local economy, providing jobs, and developing successful businesses. Russell called these organizations the "blessers." But here is the surprise. The "blessers" saw more people converted...by a ratio of 48 to 1! The lesson can be applied to our lives; the best approach is to BLESS people! Proverbs 11:25 says: Whoever brings blessing will be enriched, and one who waters will himself be watered. Here are the steps that we will discuss this week:

1. B—Begin with prayer

2. L—Listen

3. E—Engage

4. S—Serve

5. S—Story

Our first step is prayer. Ask, "God how do you want me to bless the people in the places you are already sending me?" and "Who do you want me to develop a relationship with?" Pray for the ability to recognize the opportunities that God may place in front of you each day. Whether he uses longtime relationships or a chance encounter—pray to be ready! As we will learn, God has you there for a reason. And finally, remember to create a prayer list as you begin to listen to those God leads you to. Pray for their needs as a first step of relationship building. Blessing people begins with prayer, and when God guides you, anything is possible.

## Questions to Ponder

What two things drove Paul's approach to reach lost people according to Romans 10:1? How could those two forces work to motivate you to B.L.E.S.S. others?

## Prayer

*Father, I want to seek and save the lost, just as your Son has demonstrated, but today I confess my hesitancy and fear. Forgive me and teach me ways I can reach out to make a difference in people's lives in Jesus' name. Amen.*

# Day Two: B.L.E.S.S.—Listen

*...but in humility count others more significant than yourselves.*
*Let each of you look not only to his own interests,*
*but also to the interests of others.*
*~Philippians 2:3–4 (ESV)*

*Know this, my beloved brothers: let every person be quick to*
*hear, slow to speak...*
*~James 1:19 (ESV)*

It's been said that being listened to is so close to being loved that most people cannot tell the difference. The act of setting aside yourself to enter someone else's world shows empathy, care and yes, love! Many people are looking for an ear that will listen, but they do not find it because we are wrapped up in our own interests. But what if that changed? What if we could become better listeners? What doors might open? What bridges would be built, what walls might come down? Most of us view evangelism as our turn to talk, but maybe it would be easier if we started by listening? Dietrich Bonhoeffer, the German pastor who gave his life to stand up against the Nazis in the 1940s, wrote this about the ministry of listening:

*"But Christians have forgotten that the ministry of*
*listening has been committed to them by him who*
*is himself the great listener and whose work they*
*should share. We should listen with the ears of God*
*that we may speak the Word of God."*

Our second way of blessing people is to listen. Understanding the needs of others and the places where God is at work in their lives is the first step. Before you can help others find Jesus, you need to listen to them first. What are people celebrating? What are their struggles? What are they longing for? Where do they need help? What are their questions about life?

Remember you are not trying to answer at this point, you are listening. Your goal is to make sure people are heard. Commit in every conversation to talk less and ask more questions. The more you listen and ask clarifying questions, the more opportunities you will discover to pray for those you are listening to. Lay down your assumptions, and practice being present. God can use your ears in a powerful way to communicate his love.

## Questions to Ponder

What's at the root of our struggles to listen to others according to Philippians 2:3–4? Who is a good listener that could coach you to be slow to speak and quick to listen?

## Prayer

*Father, help me through the power of your Holy Spirit to be better at the ministry of listening. Remove those attitudes in my heart that keep me from seeing others as more significant than myself so that in humility I can genuinely love by listening. Amen.*

# Day Three: B.L.E.S.S.—Engage

*When the teachers of the law who were Pharisees saw him*
*eating with the sinners and tax collectors, they asked his*
*disciples: "Why does he eat with tax collectors and sinners?"*
~Mark 2:16 (ESV)


*The Son of Man has come eating and drinking,*
*and you say, "Look at him! A glutton and a drunkard,*
*a friend of tax collectors and sinners!"*
~Luke 7:34 (ESV)

The Gospels are full of stories of Jesus eating with people. He eats with tax collectors and sinners at the home of Levi and has a meal in the home of Martha and Mary. His first miracle was done at a wedding feast. Jesus condemns the Pharisees and teachers of the law at a meal. He's at a meal when he urges people to invite the poor to their meals rather than their friends. Zacchaeus probably was taken back a bit when Jesus invites himself to dinner. There is so much more the feeding of the five thousand, the Last Supper, a meal with the two disciples in Emmaus, and cooking fish for his disciples on the shores of Galilee. No wonder the Pharisees mistook him for a glutton and drunkard! What is Jesus saying to us with his theology of food?

Something amazing happens when we engage with people socially, especially over food! Carolyn Steel wrote in her book, *Hungry City: How Food Shapes Our Lives,* "Few acts are more expressive of companionship than the shared meal... Someone with whom we share food is likely to be our friend, or well on the way to becoming one." Did you know the word "companion" comes from the Latin "cum" ("together") and "panis" ("bread")?

Our third way of blessing others is to engage, which means to participate or become involved with. Engaging another person requires you to ask this vital question: How can I spend time with this person around something that is important to them? Could you have a meal or a cup of coffee with them? A concert, sporting activity or playtime with their kids and yours? If you are listening well, you find out what will work best. More than likely, there will be a chance to have a meal as you spend time together. When we eat together, we relax and let down our guard. We can know others and be known. If you have prayed often, listened well and ask questions to dig deeper, you will find eating together a natural next step.

Look again at how Luke 7:34 describes Jesus mission strategy: he came eating and drinking! It sounds like a fun strategy don't you think? Let's put it to work!

### Question to Ponder

How could you adopt Jesus' theology of food to help you engage those you know who are far away from God?

### Prayer

*Father, thank you that through your Son you have shown us how to engage others so we might build relationships and share your love with people who are far away from you. Open my eyes to people you would like me to share a meal with so I might look, live, love and party like Jesus! Amen.*

# Day Four: B.L.E.S.S.—Serve

*For you were called to freedom, brothers.*
*Only do not use your freedom as an opportunity for the flesh,*
*but through love serve one another.*
~Galatians 5:13 (ESV)

The sitcom *Seinfeld* was famous for being a "show about nothing." In reality, each week focused on common, everyday situations... often in a hilarious way.

In one episode the main character Jerry had made friends with Keith Hernandez, a famous baseball player. Jerry was excited about this new friendship until Keith crossed what Jerry believed was an unwritten guy-friend rule: he asked Jerry to help him move! Kramer, Jerry's neighbor, agreed that Keith had stepped over the friendship line. "Before you know it he'll be asking you to drive him to the airport, too!"

When we get to know others, we will begin to see how we can serve them, our fourth way of blessing others. Sometimes, just being their friend is exactly what they need. But often we will see other ways that we can help. Maybe it's a project around the house, helping with their kids, or even... helping them move! Maybe it's just listening when they need to vent about a problem. But what-ever it is, serving gives us the chance to put our love into action. To show them that we care.

Jesus set the standard when it comes to serving. He washed his disciples' feet. He healed people's diseases. He even cooked his disciples breakfast when he appeared to them after his resurrec-tion! And most importantly of all, he served each and every one of us by giving his life on the cross to set us free from sin and death!

Paul wrote to the Galatians about this freedom we all have in Christ. But he also warned them to not use that freedom as an opportunity to serve ourselves and our own needs. We have been set free to serve others with the love we ourselves have received from God.

One writer put it this way: "People will not care what you know until they know that you care." What better way to show them that you care than by serving?

## Question to Ponder

Who can you serve in a simple but loving way today?

## Prayer

*Lord Jesus, thank you for serving me by giving your life to set me free. Help me to use my freedom to be a blessing to the others you have placed in my life. Show me how to serve them today and every day. Amen.*

# Day Five: B.L.E.S.S.—Story

*In your hearts honor Christ the Lord as holy,*
*always being prepared to make a defense to anyone*
*who asks you for a reason for the hope that is in you;*
*yet do it with gentleness and respect.*
~1 Peter 3:15 (ESV)

I was on a late flight headed home, and the seat next to me was open. I looked forward to stretching out a bit, reading my book, and probably catching a little nap. A perfect "flight plan" for a weary traveler eager to get back to his family!

Just before the door was closed on the plane, one more person hurried on board. He was big, sweaty, and headed straight for the empty seat next to me. He had a huge bag that he spent 30 seconds trying to cram into the seat in front of him, all the while practically sitting on my lap. When he finally sat down, he gave me a huge grin and loudly introduced himself. Any thought of a quiet flight was quickly left behind as we pushed back from the gate. I pushed myself against the window as best I could and braced myself for the next three hours.

As it turned out… it was an amazing flight. The guy had quite a story to tell about his life, and he told it well. The hours flew by. I was actually surprised when the pilot announced we were on our final approach into Chicago. As I got off the plane that night, I felt like I had a new friend!

We all love a good story. And if that story is true, we like it even better! Stories draw us in and hold our interest. The best stories help us get a glimpse of the big story that guides the universe and connect our own story to that big story.

Peter tells us that one of the most important ways we can honor Christ as holy is to be prepared to tell our story, the fifth way we can bless others. But not just any story… the story of Christ's work in our life. Peter calls this story "the hope that is in you." Showing someone God's love through action and service is crucial. But eventually we need to be able to tell them what God has done for us! When we do that, we connect our story, to God's big story, to the story of those around us. We give people a reason for the hope we have in Christ!

Telling your story takes practice. Peter says we have to be prepared. One resource to help you do this is, "Engaging in Story" by Saturate Resources. (https://saturatetheworld.com/resource/engaging-story-resource) God will bless the time you use to prepare your story as a blessing to help others know His story!

## Question to Ponder

Where have you seen God at work in your life, and how could you tell someone else about what God has done for you?

## Prayer

*God, help me be ready to tell the story of the hope that I have in you through your son Jesus Christ! Amen.*

# Share Your Life

*"Once we deeply trust that we ourselves are precious in God's eyes, we are able to recognize the preciousness of others and their unique places in God's heart."*
~Henri Nouwen

*"Adam's fellowship with God was perfect, and God Himself declared Adam needed other humans."*
~John Ortberg

## Introduction

It's week six! The journey we began together is about to come to an end. We have learned a lot about what it means to be disciples who make disciples. We have learned and practiced the discipleship practices used by Jesus and taught in the Word. We've spoken the truth in love. We've tested and shared our faith. And we did this with other people… people God put in our lives to help us grow more like him!

This week we turn our attention to the last and perhaps the most important discipleship topic of all—the need to live in deep, dedicated community with other believers, with love at the center of it all! On his last night before his death, as Jesus gathered his disciples he told them:

*"This is my commandment, that you love one another as I have loved you."*
~John 15:12

96

Jesus not only encouraged the disciples to love one another, he told them that by loving one another they remain in his love for them! In other words, Jesus linked the Father's love for him, his love for his disciples, and his disciples love for one another all together into one, complete package.

Christians sometimes feel like their relationship with God is distinct and separate from their relationships with other members of God's family. They desire to go deeper and deeper with Jesus, but keep others at arm's length. In this session God challenges us to open our lives to relationships, and he promises to be in the center of those relationships.

## Share

Get back together with the people you Planned with last week. Spend some time together on the following questions:

- Think of one person far from God that you encountered this week. Where did you see God at work in their life? If you had prayed for them in advance, what answer did you see to that prayer?

- If you had a chance to interact socially with someone far from God this week, how did that go? What seeds were planted? What are your next steps?

- If you had a chance to share your faith story this week, how did that go? What reaction did you get?

Once you've had a chance to share, take a moment to pray for your time together this evening.

## Hear

During the *Hear* portion of your group time this week we will hear the words of Jesus as he spoke to his disciples the night before he was betrayed, arrested, and crucified. He would never be together with them like this again! His time with them after his resurrection was different. This was the last night with them as their teacher and rabbi.

First, take a few seconds to just sit and be silent. During this time, imagine what it was like for the disciples to be with Jesus on this night, after three years of travel and sharing their lives together.

Then, have one person read the following passages:

### John 15:1–17

After the text has been read, just take another moment of silence and then play the **Session 6: Share Your Life** video.

VIDEO NOTES (FILL IN THE BLANK)

The first reason that loving one another is not easy is because

sometimes people _____ .

The second reason that loving one another is not easy is because

loving people is _____.

The final reason that loving one another is not easy is because to

love others I have to _____ with

them.

Sharing my life is worth it because God has promised it will bring

me _____.

Sharing my life is worth it because Jesus

_____ in and through me.

Sharing my life is worth it because Jesus promises _____

_____ .

## Explore

In the *Explore* section we are going to take a closer look at our theme passage itself in order to discover what it means to those who wrote and originally heard it.

1. Jesus begins this passage using the image of a gardener (his Father) and a vine (Jesus). (v. 1) Have you ever been to a vine-yard or taken a tour of a winery? What was it like? What do you remember about how the vines grow, what care they need, etc.?

2. What can we learn about the relationship between Jesus and his Father based on this image that Jesus uses?

3. As Jesus further unpacks the image, we find our place in the vineyard: we are the branches. (v. 2–8) What is the fruit that we are supposed to produce?

4. Branches that bear no fruit are cut off and discarded. But even the branches that bear fruit are pruned so that they can bear even more fruit. What might be examples of pruning in the life of believers? Can you think of a time when pruning produced even more fruitfulness in your life?

5. What is the sign to the world that we are the disciples of Jesus? How well do we do this? What would the world around us say?

6. Jesus compares his love for us to the love the Father has for him. (v. 9) Can you think of any stories in the Bible that reveal something about the Father's love for Jesus? What do these stories reveal about the love Jesus has for us?

7. Jesus commands us to love one another. (v. 12–15) He roots this command not in a master/servant relationship, but rather in our friendship with him. What's the difference?

8. What comfort do you find in verse 16 as you seek to obey the command of your friend Jesus and love others?

9. Why do you think Jesus repeats his command? (v. 17)

## Apply

In the *Apply* section we are going to get a bit more personal as we consider the implications that this text has for our own lives.

10. As a branch on Christ's vine, how would you describe the fruit that you are bearing right now? High grade? Wormy? Organic? Juicy? Unripe?

11. Sitting here today, do you feel more like a friend of Jesus or more like his servant. Why?

12. Share some ways that you have experienced the love of Jesus in your life. How could you experience more of this love from him?

13. How have you experienced God's love through others in this group? (Now would be a great time to thank them for sharing the love of Jesus with you!)

14. Who are the people that God has placed in your life to love? Without naming names, are some of them easier to love than others? Why or why not?

15. In the video we talked about a number of reasons it is hard to love others. Did these reasons make sense to you? Are there other reasons you think it is hard to love others?

16. We also explored some reasons why loving others is worth it. Which of these reasons is most exciting to you? What other reasons are there to love one another as Jesus encourages us to do?

17. How does a small group help you experience love and love others?

## Plan

During the *Plan* portion of your study you will again be encouraged to make a conscious plan to apply God's Word to your daily life based on this study.

So break into pairs or triads and share the following:

- Who specifically needs to experience God's love through you this week?
- What one, concrete growth step could you take this week...
    - To grow in your experience of Jesus and his love for you?
    - To get better at being open, willing, and able to love others?

Conclude your time of sharing in prayer for one another.

## Conclusion

Conclude your group time by coming back together as a group and reminding one another to take some time in the daily devotions during the week. Encourage one another in this process of life-long evaluation and growth!

Note that this **Apart** time is just as important as the **Together** portion of your study, as it is the place where you will continue to apply what you have learned in your daily life.

Wrap up with any important group announcements before concluding your group time. You might find a time when you can all get together one last time simply to celebrate what God has done in your group during this study! Be sure and share with one another your plans for the next trimester of group life. Your group might decide to continue meeting together, or maybe there is more than one group that could form from this group around topics of common interests. Make your plans now so you can begin to invite others to join you next trimester.

# Week Six Devotions

---

## Day One: Love God, Love Others

*One of them, an expert in the law, tested Him with a question:*
*"Teacher, which commandment is the greatest in the Law?"*
*Jesus declared, "'Love the Lord your God with all your heart*
*and with all your soul and with all your mind.' This is the first*
*and greatest commandment. And the second is like it:*
*'Love your neighbor as yourself.' All the Law and the Prophets*
*depend on these two commandments."*
*~Matthew 22:35–40*

Ever since Jim's best friend became engaged, their relationship
had been under a strain. It didn't help that Jim knew the wedding
was going to take a huge amount of time and energy for him as the
best man. But that wasn't the real issue. The real issue was this:
Jim really didn't like his best friend's fiancée.

On one hand Jim tried to convince himself it really didn't matter.
After all, *he* wasn't marrying her! He knew he and his friend would
still have their times to be together. Their friendship was still strong
even though this woman had been a part of his friend's life for a
number of years. But on the other hand, a marriage meant she
wasn't going away. Jim was going to have to learn, at some point,
to deal with her.

So, Jim made a decision. If his friend loved this woman... maybe he
could learn to love her too. Or at least like her. The next time he and
his friend were together, he asked about why he had decided to
propose. He saw the love in his friend's eyes as he talked about his
bride-to-be. He began to appreciate what his friend saw in her. He

began to see her through his eyes... and he starting to think that maybe this would all work out OK after all.

An expert in the law asks Jesus to name the greatest commandment. But Jesus throws him a little bit of a curve ball. He gives him two commandments, and links them together in a powerful way. Love God. Love others. It's as if Jesus is saying, "You can't have one without the other."

And that presents us with a problem. I'm all for loving God. But people can be hard to love sometimes! Can't I just focus on my relationship with Him... and pick and choose the people I want to love? Do I really have to love others if I am going to love God?

But when we begin to see people through Jesus' eyes, they become easier to love. If I can just remember that each and every person I meet was created in God's image and is so loved by God that he gave his life for them, then I can begin to love everyone as God commands. It isn't easy, but through God's Spirit at work in me I can indeed learn to love others has He loves them.

### Question to Ponder
Who do you know that is hard to love?

### Prayer
*Dear Lord, I know you love me so much. Let me love you in return and help me to love everyone you love. Amen.*

# Day Two: The Source of Love

*"So we have come to know and to believe the love that God
has for us. God is love, and whoever abides in love
abides in God, and God abides in him."*
*~1 John 4:16*

It was one of those "why hasn't someone come up with this before" products. The "Fontus Self-Filling Water Bottle" promised to
give bikers and hikers the convenience of a water bottle that never
needed to be refilled. It's solar panel exterior used sunlight to draw
in air and remove the water from that air. After just two hours ("in
optimum conditions") an empty bottle would be full of fresh, clear,
clean drinking water. The newspapers ran stories about the innova-
tive new product. The crowdfunding website for this new marvel
was overwhelmed with investors. In a short time over $350,000 had
been given to make the Self-Filling Water Bottle a reality. There was
only one problem: it didn't work.

The bottle was nothing more than a small dehumidifier. In moist air,
on a sunny day, the bottle could actually pull about an ounce of water out of the air... in a day. In dry air the results were far less. The
dream of a bottle that could fill itself was just that. A dream.

Many Christians seem to believe that they are "self-filling"—at least
when it comes to love. We hear God's command to love others,
and we think we have a limitless internal supply of love to use for
the task. But people are hard to love, and before we know it our
reserve tanks are empty. We just don't have enough love to go
around. So we back off a bit, give ourselves a break from loving
others, and wait for our tank to refill. On its own.

John reminds us that we do have access to an unlimited source
of love, but not from our own lives or emotional resources. God
is love. He has given that love freely to us. When we abide in that
love, God lives in us. And because God lives in us, his love is available to us whenever we need it. It is available to heal our hurts and

brokenness, and it is available to share with whoever is around us that needs that love. We become "God-filled bottles of love" that can make a real and lasting difference in the lives of others wherever and whenever it is needed.

Now *that* is something worth investing in!

## Question to Ponder

Are you seeking to share your love or God's love with others?

## Prayer

*Dear Jesus, let your love live so richly in me that it overflows in acts of love to all those I encounter every day. Amen.*

# Day Three: Love is a Choice

*"Love is patient and kind; love does not envy or boast; it is not arrogant or rude. It does not insist on its own way; it is not irritable or resentful; it does not rejoice at wrong doing, but rejoices with the truth. Love bears all things, believes all things, hopes all things, endures all things. Love never ends."*
~1 Corinthians 13:4–8a

They had been married 65 years. A local newspaper reporter asked to interview them for a feature story in the paper. As he got to know the couple he began to realize something amazing: they had very different personalities. She was outgoing and engaging. He was quiet and reserved. She laughed often and easily. He smiled quietly, and only occasionally. She shared stories of grand adventures, and of how hard she had to work to talk her husband into joining her on those adventures over the years. The reporter began to wonder, how had this relationship survived 65 months, much less 65 years?

He decided to ask. "You seem like very different people," he observed. She quickly responded, "Oh we are!" "Then, how is it that your marriage has been so successful? Why have you stayed in love all these years?" There was a moment of silence. For the first time the wife seemed to be searching for the right words. It was her husband who broke the silence. With a twinkle in his eye and a smile on his face, he answered the reporter's question. "Sometimes," he said, "love is a choice."

Paul's description of love in 1 Corinthians 13 reflects this truth. It describes love in a way that far surpasses the emotion that is sung about in love songs or that decorates the insides of Valentine's Day cards. It is patient. It is kind. It does not insist on its own way. It rejoices. It hopes. It endures. All these things do not come naturally to us as sinful, selfish human beings. For us to love like this, we must make a choice. We must choose each day to love the way God loves.

While 1 Corinthians 13 is often read at weddings, presumably to describe the love shared by the new husband and wife, it is really a description of God's love for us. God chose to love you before you were ever born. Jesus chose to love you when he willingly went to the cross for you. God's Spirit chose to love you through the waters of your Baptism. He chose us. In response, we chose to love.

**Question to Ponder**

Who can you choose to love today?

**Prayer**

*Dearest Savior, when I find myself choosing to turn away from others, give me the power to choose to love.*

# Day Four: The Father's Love

*"A voice came from heaven,*
*'You are my beloved Son; with you I am well pleased.'"*
~Mark 1:11

The video went viral in just a few days. Natalia had just gotten her learner's permit, and her dad was videoing her first attempt at driving. You can hear the pride in his voice as she flawlessly negotiates the first stop and turn. He's all smiles while she carefully maneuvers the car around the block and into their driveway. He compliments her on her driving—until she accidentally hits the gas instead of the brake and smashes the car into the family garage. "I told you to stop!" The startled father exclaims. "I did," his daughter replies.

The Bible provides us with an amazing "proud papa" moment. Jesus has been on this earth for 30 years. Other than one incident in the temple in Jerusalem when he was 12 years old, he has lived a quiet life as a carpenter in Nazareth. But now the time has come for him to begin his public ministry. He shows up by the shore of the River Jordan, ready to take the first steps on the path that will lead to a cross on a hill called Calvary, and to an empty tomb three days later! It will be a difficult journey… but it is what he came to do. It is the mission his Father sent him to accomplish. And it begins with his baptism in that river.

As he comes up from the water, we are told the heavens were "torn open." It is as if God the Father cannot contain himself. His voice booms from heaven, "You are my beloved Son; with you I am well pleased." Jesus' father acknowledges him as his son, and tells him how proud he is!

What do you think those words meant to Jesus? Were they a confirmation of all he was about to do? Did they make him long for the reunion in heaven that would take place three years later, as Jesus ascended back to his Father? Did they bring a smile to his face, and joy to his heart?

110

Because of Jesus, we have been restored as sons and daughters of that same Heavenly Father. And just as he was proud of Jesus, he is proud of us because of Jesus. Jesus said, "As the Father has loved me, so I have loved you." (John 15:9) We are loved!

## Question to Ponder

What circumstances in your life might tempt you to doubt that God loves you and is proud of you?

## Prayer

*Heavenly Father, help me to live each day in such a way that shows I know that you are proud of me. Amen.*

# Day Five: Made for Relationship

*"Then the Lord God said,*
*'It is not good that the man should be alone.'"*
~*Genesis 2:18*

On July 12, 2015, George Bell was found dead in his home, where he lived alone. His neighbors, who confessed they knew almost nothing about him, had called the police because of the odor. Police found his body on the living room floor. It was not clear how long he had been there.

To make matters worse... authorities could find no next of kin. No relatives claimed the body. No one stepped forward as a friend to tend to his remains. Apparently, he had lived as he had died. Alone.

Why does a story like that bring tears to our eyes and a sinking feeling in the pit of our stomach? Is it simply because we fear loneliness? Or is there something deeper and more profound at work here?

In Genesis we are told that God made the heavens and the earth. He crafted this universe carefully, and at each step of creation he observed what he made and proclaimed it "good." He made light and darkness. Stars, sun and moon. Land and the animals to roam on it. The sea and all the creatures that inhabit it. And human beings as the final act of his creation. "Let us make mankind in our image, after our likeness" God explained. (Genesis 1:26) But for the first time there was a problem. God looked at the man he created, and exclaimed, "It is not good for the man to be alone."

Now, he wasn't alone. Not really! God was there. But human beings were made to be like God, and God exists in relationship. Father, Son and Spirit. And God created us to be in relationship too. With God, and with others. Alone is not good. Together is what we were created for.

Throughout these six weeks we have learned about what it means to be together with God and with others. To love one another, and to help one another grow. It is hard work! But it is what we are meant to do and to be. Never, ever, alone!

## Question to Ponder

What is the one, most valuable thing God has taught you these last six weeks?

## Prayer

*Almighty God, grant me the ability each day to follow you as you lead me to love and lead others. Amen.*

# Appendix 1:
# Biblical Equipping Overview

*"All Scripture is God-breathed and is useful for teaching,
rebuking, correcting and training in righteousness,
so that the servant of God may be thoroughly equipped
for every good work."*
~2 Timothy 3:16-17 (NIV)

## What is Biblical Equipping?

Biblical Equipping is a disciplined way of encountering the Bible—by yourself and with your small group—for the purpose of hearing and understanding God's Word more clearly, knowing and loving God and others more deeply, and living for and serving God more joyfully and obediently.

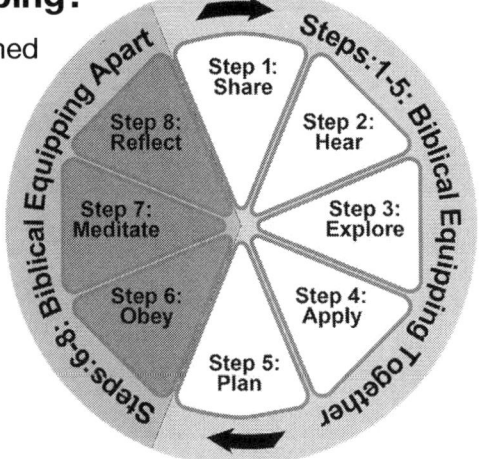

The **Together** and **Apart** components in this approach remind us that the Holy Spirit is present and active in our group gatherings. As we dive into God's Word the Holy Spirit is breathing into our lives and building us up as the Body of Christ.

God's intention for us is always woven into the complexities of life together. But the Holy Spirit doesn't depart when we get in the car and drive home. As you continue to reflect on God's Word throughout your week the Holy Spirit continues to speak to your heart and transform your thoughts and actions in ways that more fully reflect what it means to be God's child living in God's Kingdom here and now.

By following the disciplines of both the **Together** and **Apart** steps of the cycle, your group is on a path for daily contact with the Holy Spirit and the support and interaction of a community of faith built by the Spirit.

## Together

The **Together** portion is the part of your study done when you are gathered with your small group. It consists of five steps that will help guide you through an in-depth study of God's Word that is then applied to your daily life.

At the core of every discussion are really two central questions:

1. "What is God saying through this text?"
2. "What am I going to do in response?"

So let's examine each step in greater detail.

### STEP 1: SHARE

*Talk with your group about your experience in living as Jesus' disciple and how God's Word affected your life since the last group meeting.*

Though listed as the first step, it is actually the connection from the previous group session. In a way, it's the completion of the cycle you began then. You report back to the group about God's message and direction that you've experienced while **Apart.**

These sharing conversations build trust and acceptance as characteristics of your group life. Besides the hard drive you had coming to group, you might begin by sharing:

- Why a particular verse, phrase, or word from your Bible meditation during the week has become especially meaningful.
- An insight or awareness God has given as you meditated on His Word.
- A new perspective on your circumstances, relationships, or work as a result of your reflection during the week, the chal-

lenge to follow through with that perspective or the impact your action has already had.

- How a comment made by a group member at the last **Together** session remained with you through the week.

## STEP 2: HEAR

*Begin with silence to open your heart to God's Word. Then listen together as the Bible passage is read. End with silence to receive the message the Holy Spirit would give you.*

We are constantly bombarded by the noise of words, most of which are not worth being heard. In your group session you are gathered around God's Word. Honor Him by turning off the static and tuning in to God. How long your group settles into silence before reading the Word depends on your group's experience with silence and their ability to focus. It may be 15 seconds, or it may take a few minutes for the gerbil wheel in your head to come to a stop. Talk about it and try it different ways as you learn to use this tool of silence together.

For the original audience and for much of the history of God's people, the Bible was intended to be heard. Read the scripture portion for your session out loud. Group members can follow along in their Bibles or close their eyes and let God's message soak in. Hear the whole chunk and save the dissection for later. Following the reading with more silence lets the message perk in our heart rather than rushing for an immediate response.

## STEP 3: EXPLORE

*Together explore the passage in depth. Your group leader will ask focused questions to help you discover what the passage meant to those who wrote and originally heard it.*

Now you're going to dig into the particulars of the passage. You'll discuss the facts about the passage and the meaning it conveys. You might look for background information on the text or about the author, the audience, the places and context of the time. You might unpack the meaning of words or concepts used. This kind of background might come from a study guide, might be prepared by the group leader, or might be collected and shared by a member of the group gifted with knowledge and study.

Four types of questions will help you find the passage's key ideas:

- What does this passage show you about God?
- What do you learn from this passage about how God relates to people?
- What does God give or offer people?
- What kind of response to God is the passage calling for?

Let this exploration be a group effort. Balance listening, thinking, and speaking. The goal is to share ideas freely without any voice dominating or any voice never being heard. Our goal is to know God more deeply, and hearing the perspective of everyone is an excellent way to explore new facets of God. Taking notes during this discussion can be useful for further reflection during the **Apart.**

This exploring environment requires respect for each other and re-spect for God's Word. We are calling each other out to live in God's truth, yet we are asking the group to point out or own blind spots to the meaning of His Word. Be curious, intellectually honest and will-ing to go deeper. Check out related passages and footnotes. Show your group how to use a study Bible. Consider translations.

You are exploring God's Word with all of who you are, emotion-ally intellectually, physically, socially and spiritually. As you listen to group member's discussions you'll hear *facts* and *feelings.* Both are legitimate personal responses, but they both are only part of the journey to hearing God's *truth.* Be careful not to avoid the *truth* by getting stuck on either *fact* or *feeling.* Strive to be as clear and accurate as you can about the meaning of the passage.

## STEP 4: APPLY

*Apply the Bible's truth to your own life. How do those truths change the way you understand God and others? How does Jesus' teach-*

*ing and example connect with your own life? How does the Holy Spirit address your needs and challenges in this passage?*

Do you remember Connect the Dots pictures from your childhood? The details of your *Explore* discussion are best when the dots are connected into a bigger picture of application into real life. When you see what the passage means for you today, in your situation you will begin to understand how God's Word shapes and transforms our lives. Turning the corner from *Explore* in your discussion to *Connect* helps you learn what God is calling you to be and do.

Five types of questions will help you focus on issues raised by the meaning of the passage and your *Explore* discussion of it:

- *How* is God speaking directly to you as a group? To each of you individually?
- *What* is God's good news for you here?
- What is God *calling you to be* in your relationships with one another, with others outside the group, and with God?
- What is God *calling you to know?* What gracious promises is God asking you to believe and trust? What are you to understand about God and about yourselves? How will your new understandings change the way you live?
- What is God *calling you to do?* How does God want you to act? In what specific ways is God calling you to obey and to love?

Again, honest and open sharing will be an open door for God's work in the group and members' lives. Broaden your horizon by examining different arenas for your connections. Consider your connections with Trinity, your connections with each other in the group, your relationships in your personal life. As you grow to know each other and your level of transparency and trust grows you will be able to help each other make connections. Others see our situation with more objectivity than we do. They see things we miss. Just be sure all of your connections for others are governed by and delivered with love, and don't let this turn into splinter digging while you're blind to your own log. (Matthew 7:1–5)

We grow in wisdom as the Holy Spirit makes us more aware of the interconnectedness of life. The Holy Spirit leads us through the truth of Jesus' story and draws the line to our own stories. The Spirit connects our personal histories and the history of humanity. This happens in small ways through the Holy Spirit's guidance as your group grows in wisdom and understanding.

## STEP 5: PLAN

*Make a conscious plan to apply the word to your daily life. Choose a portion of the Bible passage you have just explored to concentrate on during the time between group meetings. What specific steps can you take to live by God's Word, relying on God for the strength to take those steps?*

This is where individuals get intentional and make a plan for follow through. Each group member is identifying their own plan, but as a group leader you can offer help in clarifying and being specific about steps to be taken.

The individual's plan may involve *daily obedience to God's Word* by identifying specifically how they will do that, what they will do, when they will do it. They may or may not show this plan to the group depending on their own comfort level, but encourage them to write it down for personal accountability for their action on the truth God has shown them.

The individual's plan may involve *daily attention to God's Word.* A specific action may not yet be clear, but the Spirit has been calling through the group's discussion for an individual to pay close attention to a specific portion of the passage studied or to examine other related texts. An intention to listen and watch through the week will be specific about how and when during the week you will be in contact with what portion of God's Word. Their plan may include identifying who they want to talk the passage over with.

At your session group members can make their plan alone, together as a group, or split out with partners. They may come to an agreement about making contact with a check-in during the week. The best way to help each other turn intentions into action is through prayer. As individuals share their intentions make prayer notes and pray daily for each other.

All five of these **Together** steps help us experience the fact that the Christian life is not a solo exercise. Thank God when you see group members giving each other support and encouragement as the Holy Spirit guides them to be more like Jesus. Pray that this happens in all of Trinity's small groups.

# Apart

The **Apart** is done individually by group members between group meetings. Depending on the intentions developed in the *Plan* step, individuals may move through these steps during the week or focus on one or two, but encourage people to develop in all three and to use a daily rhythm.

### STEP 6: OBEY

*Respond to God's Word by living according to what you heard and learned. Conform your thoughts to God's Word. Let it shape your behavior and the way you think about and relate to others and situations you encounter.*

You've had one group session to hear God's Word and you're clear on its meaning. Now you have a week to put the ball into play. You may be hesitant to put God's Word into action for fear you do not understand it, but God has a habit of bringing understanding through our experience of obedience.

Taking steps of obedience builds trust and frees us from doubt. You may have identified a specific action of obedience in the Prepare step or the Holy Spirit may simply whisper at a moment during the week, "Now!"

Obedience to God's Word is not confined to one point or time. Your practice of obedience brings a dynamic element into your relationship with God that is 24/7. When it springs from a loving response to the love God has extended to you, these things happen:

- You begin to do gladly what you used to avoid.
- You regularly spend time praying and being in God's presence.
- You make time to read and meditate on God's Word.
- You schedule life in order to make time for worship and praising God with your Trinity family.
- Jesus' love has empowered you to change the way you relate with another person.
- You give up a particular habit or behavior because you know it interferes with your ability to love and serve like Jesus.
- You've moved beyond thinking about obedience into actually serving in Jesus' name.

When a group member reports any of these in your *Share* step, immediately pull the group into prayers of praise for God's faithfulness in transforming individuals into the living Body of Christ.

## STEP 7: MEDITATE

*Set aside time daily to meditate. Use the portion of Bible passage you selected in Step 5, pray about it and ponder it in your heart. Connect it to what you are thinking, feeling, and experiencing. What is God revealing to you?*

Meditation involves internalizing and personalizing God's Word. You've had a good group discussion in your *Explore* step. Now chew on and digest it!

Rather than eastern meditation's depersonalization of the individual, meditation on God's Word brings a personal, even intimate connection with God. You've identified a portion, phrase or word from a passage in your *Plan* step. Follow through with meditation. You may choose a different aspect of meditation to employ each day.

# HOW TO MEDITATE

*Pray*

Ask God to be with you as you meditate. Request the Spirit's guidance and wisdom.

*Make Room for God*

Allow yourself a block of time. Enjoy this time and do not rush through it. Silence is helpful so, find a quiet place.

*Enter into the Text*

Read the portion of scripture you've chosen. Enter into the text or story as an active participant rather than a passive observer. Use your imagination as you see and hear the crowds gathered around Jesus, or see Lazarus walk out of the grave. You can read a paraphrase like *The Message.*

*Listen to the Text*

Allow God to speak through this portion of scripture. Remember the discussion your group had about it. If this is another text you have selected, try listening to the text using a Bible app. Ask yourself what this text says about God and about you.

*Internalize the Text*

Ruminate on the passage. Try memorizing it so that you can mutter it to yourself all week or write it where you'll be in contact with it periodically through the day. Paraphrase the text in your own words. Insert your name or place it in your situation. As you encounter the text again and again the Holy Spirit will give you new insight into it.

*Connect*

During your week, take time to recall the passage in all aspects of your week; on the train, in the car, at lunch, as you exercise, before you fall asleep. Look for ways to relate the passage to what's going on with you at that particular time. Think about what God is saying to you. Does God want you to take action? Is there a particular command God wants you to obey?

*Pray*

Close your time of mediation with prayer. Thank God for what He has shown you. Ask God for help with any challenging steps you are going to take.

## STEP 8: REFLECT

*Think about how God is working in your life and how you are doing at living according to God's Word. Decide what experiences you will share with others at your next group meeting.*

Your group made some good applications in your *Connect* step discussion. Now you drill down to the specifics of your life. We live at such a rapid pace that we may not even notice the steps, attitudes, decisions that got us to the present moment. We don't even know exactly what went wrong or what went right looking from God's perspective. Using reflection as a discipline helps you *remember, evaluate, and pray.* A careful examination of the events of the day can lead you to a conversation with God that is open in confessional honesty and joyful thanksgiving.

Some people find a rhythm of meditation on God's Word in the morning and reflection at the end of the day. Fueled with God's truth for the day, you are primed to follow His cues. At the end of the day it's good to look back for His footprints and be truthful about your interactions with others. This is also a good point to jot a note for next session's *Share* with your group to give witness to God's action or request specific prayer support.

# Appendix 2:
# Biblical Equipping Questions

*"Never underestimate the power of a good question."*

*~unknown*

## The Power of Good Questions

Good questions have a way of drawing us into deeper and deeper levels of reflection and life application, because they engage us in critical and self-reflective thinking.

In this Appendix we are giving you a whole host of great questions that you can ask during the *Explore* and *Apply* sections of your group study.

BUT these are also great questions that you can use during your time apart as you continue to meditate on the text throughout your week. We are simply including them here so that you always have this resource to refer to, either for this study or for any future studies you are involved in.

## Explore Questions

The purpose of *Explore* questions is to try to understand what the text meant to the person who wrote it and to those who first read it.

But you are also exploring what God is communicating through this passage. As such, these questions fall under four broad headings.

*What is God like?*

- What basic truths about God do you find in this passage?
- What does this passage teach you about Jesus? About his personality? About what is important to him?

- What does this passage show you about what God was like then? What does it tell you about what God is like now?
- What does God think in this passage?
- What do God's thoughts tell you about who God is?
- What does God feel in this passage? What do God's feelings tell you about who God is?
- What does God do in this passage? What do God's actions tell you about who God is?
- What does God say in this passage? What do God's words tell you about who God is?
- What name or names is God called in this passage? What do those names mean? What do they tell you about who God is?
- Brainstorm as many one-word descriptions as you can of God as you see him in this passage.
- What does this passage tell you about the character of God?
- How does the picture of God in this passage contradict our current cultural stereotypes about God?
- What does God do when he gets angry?
- How does this passage demonstrate God's mercy... patience... love?
- What about God in this passage surprises you?
- How does this passage change the way you think about God?
- How did God seem to change in this passage? What brought about this change?

*What Does God Want?*
- What values does God hold to in this passage?
- What is important to God in this passage?
- What does this passage teach about what it means to live as a disciple of Jesus?

*How Does God Relate to People?*
- What spiritual gifts does God give people in this passage? What does that tell you about what God is like?

- Does Jesus relate to different people in different ways in this passage? How so? How are the people different? How do their differences influence the way Jesus treats them?
- Does God relate to people differently at the end of this passage than at the beginning? To what do you attribute the differences?
- What is the situation for the people in this passage? Why do you think they are in that situation?

*How Does God Love Us?*
- What evidence of God's love do you see in this passage?
- How does God love in this passage? What does it cost God to love in this way?
- What do people do that makes God angry in this passage? How does God treat people when God gets angry?
- How did God care for people in this passage?
- How did God meet people's needs in this passage?
- Did the people in this passage deserve God's love? Why or why not? Is it possible for us to deserve God's love?

---

## Apply Questions

The purpose of *Apply* questions is to try to understand how the original meaning of the passage applies in people's lives today. Either choose questions from this list or make up your own.

We have grouped them under a few broad categories:

*God's Care*
- How does this passage help you see God's love more clearly in your own life?
- If God were like this all the time, how do you think your life would be different?
- How did God sustain this biblical character, or the people to whom this passage is written, through their time of difficulty?

How has God sustained you through times of difficulty? How do you wish God would sustain you through times of difficulty? How might God use you to help sustain others through times of difficulty?

- How does God care for people holistically (physically, emotionally, socially, intellectually, and spiritually) in this passage?
- What does God give to people in this passage? What has God given to you recently?
- How did the people in this passage trust God to meet their needs? How can you trust in similar ways?

## God's Will

- How is God challenging the person in the passage, or those to whom the passage was written? How is God challenging you in similar ways?
- What do you see in this passage that shows how God wants Christians to relate to each other? To the world? How is God calling you to relate with others differently?
- What does God give to people in this passage> What has God given to you recently?
- How is God calling you to change now? What help is God giving you to make that possible?

## God at Work in Our Lives

- How is the Spirit leading you to apply these truths to your own life?
- What lesson is there for you in this passage?
- What spiritual gifts does the Spirit give people in this passage? What does the Spirit gives those gifts? What does God expect people to do with their spiritual gifts?
- How did God respond to people's feelings, thought, words, actions in this passage? How does God respond to you when you have similar feelings, thoughts, words, actions?
- How was the character in this passage transformed? How is God transforming you right now?

- How does this passage help you understand and receive the Spirit's power and wisdom so that you can be and do what God wants?
- How does this passage teach you to communicate with God? How does it teach you to pray?
- What does our study of this passage teach you about how to study the Bible on your own?
- How did the people in this passage trust God to meet their every need? In what specific area of your life is God calling you to give up trying to run things yourself and completely trust in God's love and power?
- What was it that made it possible for the person I this passage to live in ways that pleased God? How can you live in ways that please God?
- What does this passage show you about ways you need to grow to more effectively serve God? How can this small group help you grow in those ways?
- What spiritual gifts did you learn about or see people using in this passage? What does that suggest to you about your own spiritual gifts?

*Our Response to God's Love*
- What is the question God is asking of the person in the passage? Is God asking the same question of you? If so, what is your answer?
- How did the people in this passage change their ideas about God? How does this passage cause you to change your ideas about God?
- How does this passage give you hope for the future?
- What does God want of people in this passage? What does God want of you now?
- Who is God calling you to be through this passage?
- What is God calling you to do through this passage?
- How did people in this passage obey God? What does this passage teach you about how you can obey God?

- What changes does this passage challenge to make in your life? How can the group help and support you in making those changes?
- How did the people in this passage live as witnesses to Jesus? What does this passage show you about how you can live as a witness to?
- What does God want from the people in this passage? How do, or don't, they give God what he wants? What does God want from you? How can you give God what he wants?
- How do people in this passage respond to God's love? How might you respond to God's love?
- How do people in this passage worship God? Does this passage give you any ideas about how you might worship God?
- How did the people in this passage serve God? How does their example help you choose kinds of service you might engage in? What does their service teach you about how you might serve God?
- What does this passage teach you about what it means to live as a disciple of Jesus? How do you need to grow and change in order to live as a more effective disciple of Jesus? How can this small group help you grow and change in those ways?
- How does this passage help you become more loving... peaceful... patient... kind... generous... faithful... self-controlled... ?
- How does this passage help you become more lie Jesus?
- How does this passage help you know better how to pray?
- How does this passage help you better understand and do God's will in a particular circumstance in your life right now?
- How does this passage challenge unquestioned traditions?
- What does this passage show you about how we can be more faithful followers of Jesus?

# Appendix 3: The Twelve Disciples

*"[Jesus' disciples] were perfectly ordinary in every way. They were outsiders to the religious establishment. They spanned the political spectrum...Yet with all their faults and character flaws—as remarkably ordinary as they were— these men carried on a ministry after Jesus' ascension that left an indelible impact on the world."*

~*John MacArthur,* Twelve Ordinary Men

Jesus' disciples were a surprisingly diverse group of men who went to diverse places for the sake of spreading the Gospel. Below are some brief biographical accounts of each one that give us a glimpse of who they were and the legacy they left behind.

| NAME | BIOGRAPHY |
| --- | --- |
| Simon Peter | Originally from Bethsaida, he worked as a fisherman in Capernaum. Though very pious, he was not trained in the Law (see Acts 4:13). Eventually became the leader of the Twelve and the head of the church in Jerusalem. Authored the letters of 1 & 2 Peter and is a prominent character in the book of Acts. He was martyred in Rome sometime between 62 & 65 AD, crucified upside down. |
| James, the son of Zebedee | Brother of John and one of Jesus' inner circle. Was a fisherman by trade, working under his father and alongside his brother. Went on to become a leader of the church in Jerusalem and was one of the first martyrs, being killed by Herod Agrippa I in AD 44. |
| John, the son of Zebedee | A fisherman by trade, he too became a part of Jesus' inner circle. John became an important leader for the church in Ephesus and even helped train some of the prominent Christian leaders and martyrs of the 2nd century. He eventually went on to author the Gospel of John, three epistles (1, 2, and 3 John), and possibly even the book of Revelation. The only disciple to die in old age. |
| Andrew | Originally a disciple of John the Baptist, he was also the brother of Simon Peter. It was Andrew who introduced Peter to Jesus. He was martyred in Achaia for sharing his faith. |
| Philip | Called as one of the earliest disciples of Jesus, he is also responsible for introducing Nathaniel/Bartholomew to Jesus. Philip also partnered with Andrew in bringing some Greeks to meet Jesus in John 12:21. Tradition says he went on to become one of the first bishops in the province of Asia and is buried along with his daughters in Hieropolis. He was crucified for healing and converting the wife of the local proconsul to Christianity, and tradition states that even from the cross he was preaching forgiveness to all through Christ Jesus. |

| NAME | BIOGRAPHY |
|------|-----------|
| Bartholomew | Also known as Nathaniel, he was one of the earliest disciples of Jesus. Not much is known about Bartholomew as he is rarely mentioned in the New Testament. Tradition states that he went on to bring the Gospel to India where he was martyred by the brother of a local ruler for converting him to the faith. |
| Matthew | Also known as Levi, he was a tax collector serving the Roman government before becoming a disciple of Jesus. A gifted writer and student of the Old Testament, he is credited with writing the Gospel of Matthew. He is credited by church tradition as being a gifted evangelist of the Jews in Judaea before moving on to other countries. He is believed to have been martyred in Ethiopia for standing up to a corrupt king. |
| Thomas | Also known as "Doubting Thomas" he was the last of the Twelve disciples to see the risen Christ. Nevertheless, Thomas went further than any of the other apostles to spread the Gospel, traveling to the southern tip of India and founding a Christian community that continues to this day. He was martyred AD 72 by King Vasudeva I of the Kushan Empire. |
| James, the son of Alphaeus | Again, little is known about James the son of Alphaeus beyond his name and inclusion with the Twelve. Church tradition says that he was stoned to death and was buried near the Temple in Jerusalem for preaching Jesus as the Messiah. |
| Thaddaeus | Also known as Jude, very little is known about him from the New Testament. Church tradition says he was originally a disciple of John the Baptist, having traveled from his home in Syria to hear John preach. He then became a disciple of Jesus. After the ascension he returned to Syria and later went on to spread the Gospel throughout Mesopotamia and Persia. Tradition also credits him with healing King Abgar of Osroene and converting him to Christianity. He was martyred by beheading alongside Simon the Zealot for his missionary work. |
| Simon the Zealot | A member of a violent nationalist group called the Zealots, Simon would have considered all Romans and their collaborators enemies and would have looked down on non-Jews as outsiders. However, church tradition credits him with joining Thaddaeus in taking the Gospel throughout Syria, Mesopotamia, and Persia, where he was eventually sawn in half for his missionary efforts. |
| Judas Iscariot | Perhaps one of the more (in)famous disciples, Judas was tasked with managing the funds for Jesus' missionary efforts. He later betrayed Jesus to the High Priest for the price of 30 pieces of silver. When he learned that Jesus was to be condemned to death he attempted to return the money to the high priest but was rejected. He committed suicide by hanging as a result. |

# Unity in Diversity

*"We have a powerful myth in our culture,*
*the myth of the self-made man or woman.*
*But let's be honest. There's no such thing.*
*Success requires help—and usually lots of it."*

~Michael Hyatt

## Introduction—Leader Information

Welcome to your first study as a group! Over the next several weeks we are going to be talking about the importance of discipleship and learning what it means to look, live, and love more like Jesus.

But this is not a journey that we embark on alone. We need to be together in community. Why? Because that's the way God designed it. In fact, Solomon wrote the following about the importance of community.

*"Two are better than one, because they have a good*
*reward for their labor. If either of them falls down,*
*one can help the other up. But pity anyone who*
*falls and has no one to help them up...Though one*
*may be overpowered, two can defend themselves.*
*A cord of three strands is not easily broken."*

~Ecclesiastes 4:9–12

And this is where your group comes in. Over the next several weeks you will have a chance to get to know one another better, encourage each other in your respective walks with Jesus, and grow in your understanding of what it means to be His disciples.

But doing life together is not always easy. It will involve honest conversations, vulnerability, a readiness to listen, and perhaps even a bit of conflict. But that's okay. That is also how God designed it. Which is why this first study is going to focus on the theme of diversity and what it really means to live life together in community.

## Share

*Materials:* Object to pass around (ball, cross, stuffed animal, etc.)

*Purpose:* To spend time in relationship with peers.

**Step 1:** Have the students sit in one big circle.

**Step 2:** Explain that the only student who gets to SHARE their answer is the one holding the object. Students will likely need you to remind them throughout the process.

**Step 3:** Ask the students what they did today or this last week. Pass the object around the circle.

**Step 4:** Ask the students what good things happened this week. Pass the object around the circle.

**Step 5:** Ask the students what bad or hard things happened this week. Pass the object around the circle.

**Step 6:** Ask the students to share their favorite _____ (leader choice). Pass the object around the circle.

## Hear

*Materials: The Jesus Storybook Bible,* timer

*Purpose:* To listen to God's Word together.

**Step 1:** Gather the students in one area to sit and listen.

**Step 2:** Read the Bible event titled "Let's Go!" beginning on page 208 of *The Jesus Storybook Bible.*

**Step 3:** Stop while reading to ask questions, look at the pictures and discuss what you are talking about.

**Step 4:** Have the students close their eyes and stay still while you set a timer for 15–30 seconds (depending upon the age group of the children). During this time the students should THINK about what they just heard.

## Explore

*Materials:* Fishers of Men worksheet (one per child), writing supplies, Bible (not picture Bible)

*Purpose:* To help students learn about the diversity of the disciples.

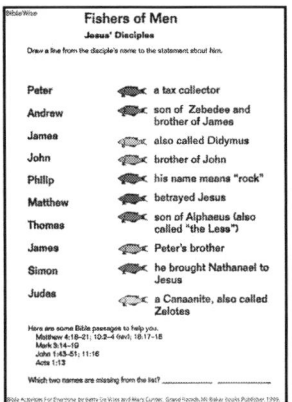
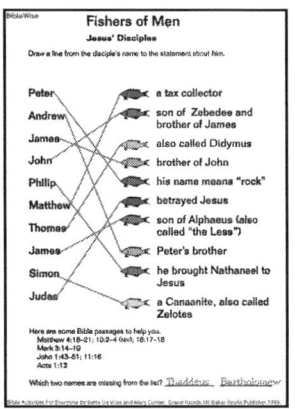

**Step 1:** Transition students to a table with the worksheet copies, writing supplies and at least one regular Bible.

**Step 2:** Explain that we are going to connect the names on the left to the phrases describing people on the right.

**Step 3:** Read the suggest passages one at a time to the group. When an answer is revealed in the text, guide the students to connect the name and phrase.

# Apply

*Materials:* Paper Doll Outlines copied on white cardstock (one per child), coloring supplies

*Purpose:* To help students see what they look like.

**Step 1:** Transition students to a table with the paper copies and coloring supplies.

**Step 2:** Explain that we are going to color these dolls to look like ourselves. Think about things like hair color, eye color, skin color, height, and clothing style. What other objects do you usually have with you that you can draw in the open space?

**Step 3:** Help the students to create their self-image dolls.

**Step 4:** Place all the pictures next to each other

**Step 5:** Discuss the following questions:

- What do they have in common? (Look for colors, objects, styles, etc.)

- What is different? (Look for colors, objects, styles, etc.)

- What does God see when he looks at each of us?

# Plan

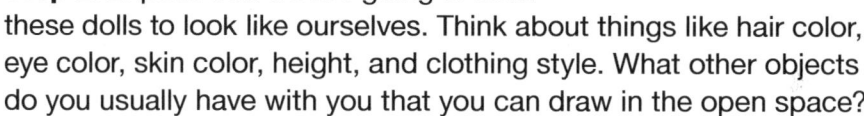

*Materials:* several mirrors

*Purpose:* To help student reflect their faces to others.

**Step 1:** Pass out mirrors or lay them on the floor of your space.

**Step 2:** Have students take turns looking at themselves.

**Step 3:** Ask the students to make different faces while looking at themselves in the mirror. (Angry, Happy, Sad, Excited, Annoyed, Frustrated, Loving, etc.)

**Step 4:** Ask the students to think about what type of face they should make in different situations. Below are some sample situations to use, but please come up with your own or use ones relevant to the students.

- My brother stole my toy.
- I'm singing *Jesus Loves Me.*
- I fell down the stairs.
- I got the birthday present I wanted.
- I hit the ball at my baseball/softball game.
- I scored the winning goal!
- My dog peed on my bed.
- I have to clean my room.

End with:

- I am telling my friends about Jesus.

**Step 5:** Remind the students that they should always be happy and smiling when they are talking to their friends about Jesus. Just because they don't look just like you or have the same interests, doesn't mean you can't tell them about Jesus.

**Step 6:** Have the students pick one friend they can say "Jesus love you" to this week.

---

# Pray

*Materials:* None

*Purpose:* To spend time in conversation with God.

As an echo prayer, have the students repeat each phrase after you:

*Dear God, thank you for loving me. Thank you for making each of us special. Help me to tell other people how much you love them. Help me to LOOK like you! You are amazing! Amen!*

# Speaking the Truth in Love

*"Handle them carefully, for words have more power
than atom bombs."*

~Pearl Strachan Hurd

---

## Introduction—Leader Information

Words have power. In fact, author and speaker Yehuda Berg once wrote:

*"Words are singularly the most powerful force
available to humanity. We can choose to use this
force constructively with words of encouragement, or
destructively using words of despair."*

In this session we are going to talk about the power of words and the role they can have either in helping or hindering our walk with Christ.

But before we dive into our study, let's take a moment to share what God has been doing in our lives this past week.

---

## Share

*Materials:* Object to pass around (ball, cross, stuffed animal, etc.)

*Purpose:* To spend time in relationship with peers.

**Step 1:** Have the students sit in one big circle.

**Step 2:** Explain that the only student who gets to SHARE their answer is the one holding the object. Students will likely need you to remind them throughout the process.

**Step 3:** Ask the students what they did today or this last week. Pass the object around the circle.

**Step 4:** Ask the students what good things happened this week. Pass the object around the circle.

**Step 5:** Ask the students what bad or hard things happened this week. Pass the object around the circle.

**Step 6:** Ask the students to share their favorite _____ (leader choice). Pass the object around the circle.

## Hear

*Materials: The Jesus Storybook Bible,* timer

*Purpose:* To listen to God's Word together.

**Step 1:** Gather the students in one area to sit and listen.

**Step 2:** Read the Bible event titled "Going Home" beginning on page 318 of *The Jesus Storybook Bible.*

**Step 3:** Stop while reading to ask questions, look at the pictures and discuss what you are talking about.

**Step 4:** Ask the students what God told the disciples to do.

**Step 5:** Have the students close their eyes and stay still while you set a timer for 15–30 seconds (depending upon the age group of the children). During this time the students should THINK about what they just heard.

## Explore

*Materials:* honesty target worksheets, coloring supplies

*Purpose:* To help students understand what honesty is and why it is important.

**Step 1:** Transition the students to a table with coloring supplies and copies.

**Step 2:** If any students can read, have them read the target phrases. If not, you will need to read to the students.

**Step 3:** Let the students color their targets.

**Step 4:** Teach the students the motions or movements to help them remember what honesty is.

- I will tell the truth (Thumb points in towards yourself)

- I will tell the truth (Thumb points in towards yourself)

- Saying what is right and true (Hands around mouth like shouting)

- I will tell the truth (Thumb points in towards yourself)

**Step 5:** Read the phrase together as a group at least ivef times and use the motions.

## Apply

*Materials:* honest sign, dishonest sign, list of situations

*Purpose:* To help students self-identify the importance of being honest.

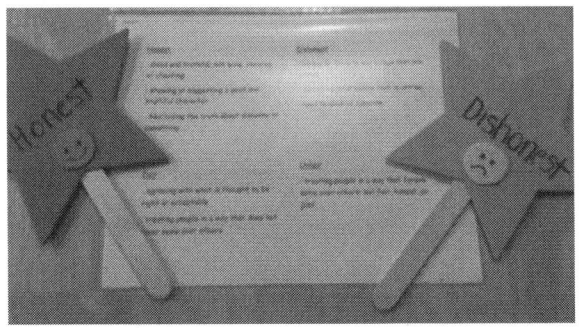

**Step 1:** Place the signs on opposite sides of the room.

**Step 2:** Explain to the students what HONEST means.

**Step 3:** Explain to the students what DISHONEST means.

**Step 4:** Read a situation, you can add your own too, and instruct the student to move to the sign that goes with the statement. You can add additional statements relevant to your group of students.

- Jesus loves me
- Jesus died for SOME of us
- If I know someone cheated on their homework, I should tell the teacher.
- I blamed the dog for stealing the cake, but I did it.
- Jesus didn't rise from the dead.
- I said I didn't know who broke mom's flowers, but I knocked them off the table.

**Step 5:** Explain to the students how important it is to be honest. This includes telling the truth about Jesus and sometimes telling people things they don't want to hear.

## Plan

*Materials:* pre-cut hands, writing supplies

*Purpose:* To help student focus their thoughts and prayers on specific people.

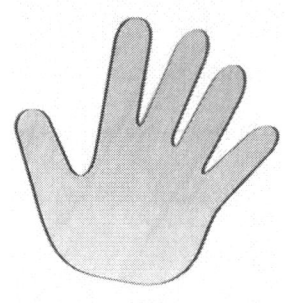

**Step 1:** Gather students at the table.

**Step 2:** Remind the students what God told us to do in the Bible event. We are supposed to GO and make more disciples.

**Step 3:** Pass out one hand to each student.

**Step 4:** Ask the student to draw a picture or write the name of someone specific they want to pray for to know Jesus.

**Step 5:** If students have more than one person, pass out more hands.

**Step 6:** Remind students to take these hands home and pray for these people every single day.

---

# Pray

*Materials:* hands from plan time

*Purpose:* To spend time in conversation with God.

As an echo prayer, have the students repeat each phrase after you:

> *Dear God, thank you for sending Jesus. Help me to tell your truth to other people. We pray for _____ (Say the names written on the hands). We want them to know you. You are amazing! Amen!*

# Test Your Faith

*"Courage is not simply one of the virtues,*
*but the form of every virtue at the testing point."*
~C.S. Lewis

*"Testing leads to failure,*
*and failure leads to understanding."*
~Burt Rutan

## Introduction—Leader Information

You've made it to week three in our study together! As we have studied the importance of becoming disciples that make disciples, so far we have learned that growth happens best in a diverse community dedicated to helping one another grow. And we've learned the importance of speaking the truth in love in that community.

This week we turn our attention to another important discipleship topic—the need to test our faith. The Apostle Paul wrote:

*"Examine yourselves to see whether you are in the*
*faith; test yourselves. Do you not realize that Christ*
*Jesus is in you—unless, of course, you fail the test?"*
~2 Corinthians 13:5

Tests can be frightening things. "Test anxiety" is a reality for many people! Add to this the idea the fact that Paul warns us that failing the test can put our relationship with Jesus in question, and the stakes are high!

But we will find this week that testing is an important part of growth. God is not trying to fail you! In fact, he knows that through examining our faith in the community of our Christian family, we can grow more and more like Jesus and become the disciples he created us to be.

## Share

*Materials:* Object to pass around (ball, cross, stuffed animal, etc.)

*Purpose:* To spend time in relationship with peers.

**Step 1:** Have the students sit in one big circle.

**Step 2:** Explain that the only student who gets to SHARE their answer is the one holding the object. Students will likely need you to remind them throughout the process.

**Step 3:** Ask the students what they did today or this last week. Pass the object around the circle.

**Step 4:** Ask the students what good things happened this week. Pass the object around the circle.

**Step 5:** Ask the students what bad or hard things happened this week. Pass the object around the circle.

**Step 6:** Ask the students who they prayed for from last week's hand prints. Pass the object around the circle.

**Step 7:** Did anyone get to talk to the person they were praying for about Jesus?

## Hear

*Materials: The Jesus Storybook Bible,* timer.

*Purpose:* To listen to God's Word together.

**Step 1:** Gather the students in one area to sit and listen.

**Step 2:** Read the Bible events titled "God to the Rescue!" and "God Makes a Way" beginning on page 84 of *The Jesus Storybook Bible.*

**Step 3:** Stop while reading to ask questions, look at the pictures and discuss what you are talking about.

**Step 4:** Ask the students what it felt like for the Israelites throughout this story. If younger, you can have the students make faces to describe how they felt instead of using words.

**Step 5:** Have the students close their eyes and stay still while you set a timer for 15–30 seconds (depending upon the age group of the children). During this time the students should THINK about what they just heard.

---

## Explore

*Materials:* Pre-made blue gelatin in a 9″ x 13″ glass pan, small paper plates/bowls, spoons, plastic knife, small people figurines

*Purpose:* Help students to visualize what it looked like for the Israelites to TRUST God.

**Step 1:** Make the gelatin a day in advance and keep it refrigerated until right before use.

**Step 2:** Transition the students to the table where they can all see the container.

**Step 3:** Utilize the small people figurines to retell the Bible event in your own words. When you get to the part where the water splits, use the plastic knife to literally cut the middle out creating a path.

**Step 4:** Have each child take a turn "walking" a figuring through the path.

**Step 5:** While walking the figurines, discuss how they would have needed to trust God to keep them safe.

**Step 6:** The remaining gelatin can be served as a snack if no allergies exist in the group.

---

# Apply

*Materials:* Armor of God coloring sheet, coloring supplies, regular Bible

*Purpose:* To help students feel confident in their faith.

Armor of God

SALVATION

SPIRIT

FAITH

RIGHTEOUSNESS

TRUTH

THE GOSPEL OF PEACE

Ephesians 6:11-18

**Step 1:** Transition students to a clean space with coloring supplies and copies of the armor of God coloring sheet.

**Step 2:** Walk through each of the components with the students and color them one at a time. **\*\*Do the shield of faith LAST.\*\***

**Step 3:** Explain to the students how important the shield of faith is. Without our faith in God, we lose everything. We need to stay con-**nected to him by believing in all he has done for us.**

**Step 4:** Using the regular Bible, read Ephesians 6:11–18.

# Plan

*Materials:* Family Values poster, writing supplies

*Purpose:* To help the students reflect on their personal relationship with God.

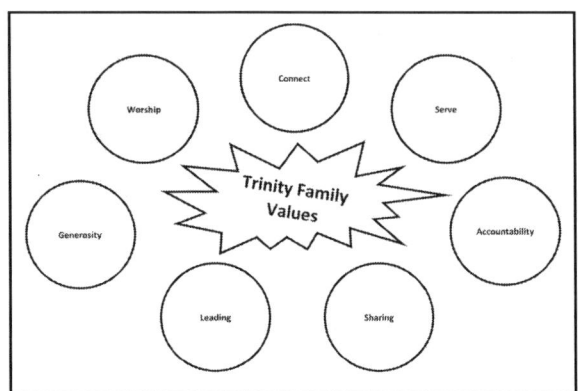

**Step 1:** Pass out writing supplies to each student

**Step 2:** Walk the students through each of the Family Values and make sure they understand what the words mean.

**Step 3:** Work together to draw pictures, symbols or words that represent each of the Family Values in the space near the words.

**Step 4:** Remind the students that we should each be working on these Family Values every single day.

# Pray

*Materials:* hands from plan time

*Purpose:* To spend time in conversation with God.

As an echo prayer, have the students repeat each phrase after you:

*Dear God, thank you for sending Jesus. I believe in Him. I trust you to take care of me. Help me to look, live and love more like Jesus. You are amazing! Amen!*

# Try and Discuss

*"God doesn't call people who are qualified. He calls people who are willing and then qualifies them."*

~Richard Parker

*"In most every business, you learn by doing. The apprenticeship model is much more effective than the classroom for cultivating entrepreneurs."*

~Andrew Yang

---

## Introduction—Leader Information

We have discovered in past weeks that an environment of diversity, honest conversations, and fearless self-evaluation creates a safe place for disciples to grow in their faith. While Jesus' disciples never received what we would think of as formal training, they became incredibly capable leaders in the early church. A key to their success was the way Jesus taught them to practice new behaviors. Jesus showed them what to do, discussed the "why's" of the teaching, and then he sent them out to do ministry without his direct involvement.

*And he called the twelve and began to send them out two by two...*

~Mark 6:7

This week we will learn how to replicate Jesus' hands on, try it out, talk about it way of teaching. Our goal is to first learn by being taught using Jesus' try and discuss method. As we experience learning that compels us to put knowledge into action, we will also learn to use Jesus' method to teach others. Mastering Jesus' method of teaching is another important step in becoming a disciple that make disciples.

## Share

*Materials:* Object to pass around (ball, cross, stuffed animal, etc.)

*Purpose:* To spend time in relationship with peers.

**Step 1:** Have the students sit in one big circle.

**Step 2:** Explain that the only student who gets to SHARE their answer is the one holding the object. Students will likely need you to remind them throughout the process.

**Step 3:** Ask the students what they did today or this last week. Pass the object around the circle.

**Step 4:** Ask the students what good things happened this week. Pass the object around the circle.

**Step 5:** Ask the students what bad or hard things happened this week. Pass the object around the circle.

**Step 6:** Ask the students which Trinity Family Value they worked on this last week. Pass the object around the circle.

**Step 7:** Did anyone get to talk to the person they were praying for about Jesus?

## Hear

*Materials: The Jesus Storybook Bible,* timer

*Purpose:* To listen to God's Word together.

**Step 1:** Gather the students in one area to sit and listen.

**Step 2:** Read the Bible event titled "The Friend of Little Children" beginning on page 256 of *The Jesus Storybook Bible.*

**Step 3:** Stop while reading to ask questions, look at the pictures and discuss what you are talking about.

**Step 4:** Ask the students, "What does it feel like when someone doesn't listen to you?"

**Step 5:** Have the students close their eyes and stay still while you set a timer for 15–30 seconds (depending upon the age group of the children). During this time the students should THINK about what they just heard.

---

## Explore

*Materials:* plastic tablecloth or newspaper, white cardstock, white crayons, water color paints, paint brushes, paper cup/bowl, water

*Purpose:* To help students understand that things like faith and a relationship for Jesus is there even when you can't see it.

**Step 1:** Put down a plastic tablecloth or newspaper on the table and fill cups or bowls with water.

**Step 2:** Pass out one piece of white cardstock to each student and put white crayons on the table.

**Step 3:** Have the students draw a cross or write a phrase like "Jesus Loves Me" on the paper using the white crayon.

**Step 4:** Explain that we can't really see the white crayon, just like we can't see the Holy Spirit in the hearts of our friends and they can't see him inside of us.

**Step 5:** Have the students dip paintbrushes in water and then the water colors to cover their entire sheet of paper with paint.

**Step 6:** Ask the students what happens when you paint over the crayon? How is this like when sin? (When we sin and ask for forgiveness the sin can't stick to our hearts because of our relationship with God.)

**Step 7:** Place these somewhere to dry with each student's name.

# Apply

*Materials:* none

*Purpose:* To help students feel more comfortable talking about Jesus.

**Step 1:** Have the students stand in a circle.

**Step 2:** Have the students repeat each phrase after you, until they have it memorized. It will probably be helpful to have them create movements or motions.

- Jesus Loves You!
- Jesus Wants You!
- Jesus Keeps You Safe!
- Jesus Died for You!
- God Forgives You!

**Step 3:** Have the students share their favorite one of these phrases with the group.

# Plan

*Materials:* none

*Purpose:* To get the students comfortable talking about Jesus.

**Step 1:** Split the students up into pairs or groups of three.

**Step 2:** Have them practice saying the phrases to each other.

- Jesus Loves You!
- Jesus Wants You!
- Jesus Keeps You Safe!
- Jesus Died for You!
- God Forgives You!

**Step 3:** Ask the students to think of one person they will try to say one of the phrases to this next week.

---

# Pray

*Materials:* hands from plan time

*Purpose:* To spend time in conversation with God.

As an echo prayer, have the students repeat each phrase after you:

*Dear God, thank you for sending Jesus. Help me, to talk to my friends about you. You love us and forgive us. You are amazing! Amen!*

# Witness—
# Sharing Our Faith

*"I do not know anything that would wake up Chicago better than for every man and woman here who loves Him to begin to talk about Him to their friends, and just to tell them what He has done for you. You have got a circle of friends. Go and tell them of Him."*

~Dwight L. Moody

## Introduction—Leader Information

In this fifth week of our study, we will be encouraging one another to grow in our witness to others for Jesus. Often Christians are hesitant and even fearful of discussing this essential part of our faith, but we shouldn't let fear keep us from this topic! A witness provides evidence or testimony to convince others of the truth. As Christians, we are called to provide evidence of who Jesus is, what he has done for humanity, and what it means to follow him. Our witness foundational to every Christian's identity—it is not an optional activity of our faith. The question that we must ask ourselves is, "What does my life say to others about Jesus?"

While our witness begins with our behaviors, it doesn't end there. Maybe you have heard the quip, "Preach the Gospel at all times. Use words when necessary!" This statement highlights the importance of our behaviors, but it misses the point of the Gospel. Jesus is our model for behavior, "the Word made flesh." He spoke the truth about who God is, identifying the problem of sin and how his death and resurrection are the only solution to this problem that has the power to separate people from God forever. Our behavior

152

and our words are both required to share this good news with others as Jesus instructed us in the Great Commission.

Jesus promises the Holy Spirit's presence and power in order for us to witness to the world.

> *But you will receive power when the Holy Spirit has come upon you, and you will be my witnesses in Jerusalem and in all Judea and Samaria, and to the end of the earth."*
> *~Acts 1:8*

Remember our mission statement is to look, live and love more like Jesus. The Holy Spirit's power will shape our behaviors, but he will also do for us what he has done for millions of Christians that have gone before us, he will help us give a verbal testimony of faith and the ability to speak when the right moment presents itself. Are you ready to experience the work of the Holy Spirit? You will sense his power and presence as you are a witness for Jesus!

## Share

*Materials:* Object to pass around (ball, cross, stuffed animal, etc.)

*Purpose:* To spend time in relationship with peers.

**Step 1:** Have the students sit in one big circle.

**Step 2:** Explain that the only student who gets to SHARE their answer is the one holding the object. Students will likely need you to remind them throughout the process.

**Step 3:** Ask the students what they did today or this last week. Pass the object around the circle.

**Step 4:** Ask the students what good things happened this week. Pass the object around the circle.

**Step 5:** Ask the students what bad or hard things happened this week. Pass the object around the circle.

**Step 6:** Ask the students who they talked to about God this last week.

# Hear

*Materials: The Jesus Storybook Bible,* timer

*Purpose:* To listen to God's Word together.

**Step 1:** Gather the students in one area to sit and listen.

**Step 2:** Read the Bible event titled "Treasure Hunt!" beginning on page 250 of *The Jesus Storybook Bible.*

**Step 3:** Stop while reading to ask questions, look at the pictures and discuss what you are talking about.

**Step 4:** Ask the students what the treasure was.

**Step 5:** Have the students close their eyes and stay still while you set a timer for 15–30 seconds (depending upon the age group of the children). During this time the students should THINK about what they just heard.

# Explore

*Materials:* white paper, adult scissors, cotton balls, white glue, cotton swabs, rainbow ribbon or crepe paper, marker, tape

*Purpose:* To remind students that God is always there with them.

**Step 1:** Pre-cut cloud shapes out of the white paper and write "God's Promise" on them.

**Step 2:** Help the students to pull the cotton balls apart to make them bigger and fluffier.

**Step 3:** Help the students use the white glue to attach the cotton balls to the cloud.

**Step 4:** Pre-cut the ribbon or crepe paper into 18″ lengths.

**Step 5:** Tape the rainbow pieces to the back of the cloud.

**Step 6:** Remind the students that God is with them every single day. Even when it is difficult to talk about your relationship with him, you need to stand firm.

---

## Apply

*Materials:* copies of Bible verse cards on card stock, coloring supplies, hole punch, rings, student scissors

*Purpose:* To help the students get into the word.

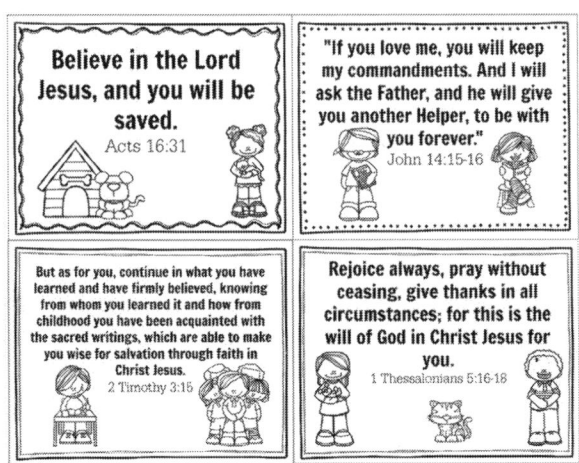

**Step 1:** Gather students at a table with coloring supplies and copies.

**Step 2:** Read through each of the verses with the students as they color them.

**Step 3:** Pass out student scissors to the students so they can cut out each card.

**Step 4:** Punch a hole in the same spot on each card.

**Step 5:** Put the cards on the ring.

## Plan

*Materials:* Salvation Verse Cards

*Purpose:* To give the students a tool to talk about Jesus.

**Step:** Challenge the students to give their verse cards away to other people. They should choose people they already know.

## Pray

*Materials:* hands from plan time

*Purpose:* To spend time in conversation with God.

As an echo prayer, have the students repeat each phrase after you:

*Dear God, thank you for sending Jesus. Help me to share your words with my friends. You know what they need to hear. You are with me always. You are amazing! Amen!*

# Share Your Life

*"Once we deeply trust that we ourselves are precious in God's eyes, we are able to recognize the preciousness of others and their unique places in God's heart."*
~Henri Nouwen

*"Adam's fellowship with God was perfect, and God Himself declared Adam needed other humans."*
~John Ortberg

## Introduction—Leader Information

It's week six! The journey we began together is about to come to an end. We have learned a lot about what it means to be disciples who make disciples. We have learned and practiced the discipleship practices used by Jesus and taught in the Word. We've spoken the truth in love. We've tested and shared our faith. And we did this with other people... people God put in our lives to help us grow more like him!

This week we turn our attention to the last and perhaps the most important discipleship topic of all—the need to live in deep, dedicated community with other believers, with love at the center of it all! On his last night before his death, as Jesus gathered his disciples he told them:

*"This is my commandment, that you love one another as I have loved you."*
~John 15:12

Jesus not only encouraged the disciples to love one another, he told them that by loving one another they remain in his love for them! In other words, Jesus linked the Father's love for him, his love for his disciples, and his disciples love for one another all together into one, complete package.

Christians sometimes feel like their relationship with God is distinct and separate from their relationships with other members of God's family. They desire to go deeper and deeper with Jesus, but keep others at arm's length. In this session God challenges us to open our lives to relationships, and he promises to be in the center of those relationships.

## Share

*Materials:* Object to pass around (ball, cross, stuffed animal, etc.)

*Purpose:* To spend time in relationship with peers.

**Step 1:** Have the students sit in one big circle.

**Step 2:** Explain that the only student who gets to SHARE their answer is the one holding the object. Students will likely need you to remind them throughout the process.

**Step 3:** Ask the students what they did today or this last week. Pass the object around the circle.

**Step 4:** Ask the students what good things happened this week. Pass the object around the circle.

**Step 5:** Ask the students what bad or hard things happened this week. Pass the object around the circle.

**Step 6:** Ask the students who they talked to about God this last week.

## Hear

*Materials: The Jesus Storybook Bible,* timer

*Purpose:* To listen to God's Word together.

**Step 1:** Gather the students in one area to sit and listen.

**Step 2:** Read the Bible event titled "God Sends Help" beginning on page 326 of *The Jesus Storybook Bible.*

**Step 3:** Stop while reading to ask questions, look at the pictures and discuss what you are talking about.

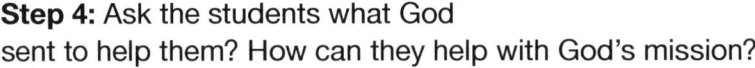

**Step 4:** Ask the students what God sent to help them? How can they help with God's mission?

**Step 5:** Have the students close their eyes and stay still while you set a timer for 15–30 seconds (depending upon the age group of the children). During this time the students should THINK about what they just heard.

## Explore

*Materials:* card stock copies of cross on sheet, white glue, cotton swabs, miscellaneous puzzle pieces, Bibles

*Purpose:* To see how Jesus helps us through His Word.

**Step 1:** Read the following verses to describe how Jesus helps us:

- Romans 12:18 (Peace)
- Romans 10:13 (Save)
- John 8:32 (Truth)
- Psalm 16:11 (Joy)
- Jeremiah 29:11 (Hope)

Add additional verses if you would like.

**Step 2:** Verse by verse write the key words on puzzle pieces (one per child).

**Step 3:** Help the student attach the puzzle pieces to their cross so the words can be seen.

**Step 4:** Write the students names on their sheets.

---

# Apply

*Materials:* Copies of puzzle pieces on regular paper, poster board, markers, crayons, glue stick

*Purpose:* To help students understand how we are all connected.

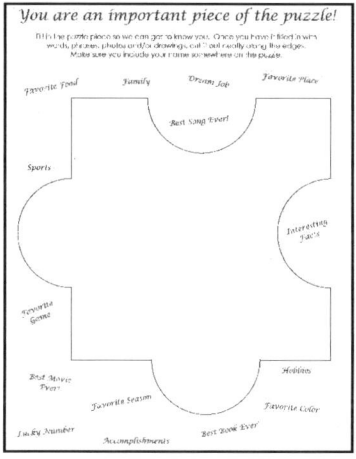

**Step 1:** Gather students around a table.

**Step 2:** Pre-cut out the puzzle pieces (one per child).

**Step 3:** Help the students draw pictures of or write words to describe themselves.

**Step 4:** Put the pieces together on the poster to connect the students.

**Step 5:** Explain that although we all have different interests, we are all connected by God's mission for our lives and his love for us. We need to work to look, live and love like Jesus!

## Plan

*Materials: Jesus is the Light* signs, hole punch, glow stick bracelets or necklaces (2 per child)

*Purpose:* To give students something to share with others.

**Step 1:** Pre-cut and hole punch the signs.

**Step 2:** Gather students in a circle.

**Step 3:** Open package of glow sticks to make sure the connectors are attached to each stick.

**Step 4:** Explain to the students that one of these is for them and the other one is to give to a friend to share Jesus' light with them.

**Step 5:** Help the students to assemble their glow stick with card to give away to someone else.

## Pray

*Materials:* hands from plan time

*Purpose:* To spend time in conversation with God.

As an echo prayer, have the students repeat each phrase after you:

> *Dear God, thank you for sending Jesus. He is the light of the world. I want to share my life with Jesus. Thank you for being with me always. You are amazing! Amen!*

Printed in Great Britain
by Amazon

74203551R00095